'Tis a Pity She's a Whore

John Ford

Dalcassian
Publishing
Company

PHILADELPHIA, PA

'Tis a Pity She's a Whore

The text is derived from The Dramatic Works of John Ford, with notes critical and explanatory, by William Gifford, published by John Murray in 1827.

Library of Congress Cataloging-in-Publication Data

'Tis a Pity She's a Whore

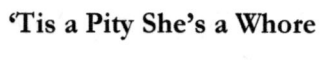

'Tis a Pity She's a Whore

Table of Contents
Preface.
Dramatis Personæ.

This tragedy, in the dedication to the Earl of Peterborough, is styled, “the first fruits of the author’s leisure.” How long it had been written, or what was the date of its first appearance, is nowhere mentioned; but it was given to the press in 1633, with the following title: “’Tis Pity She’s a Whore; acted by the Queenes Majesties seruants, at the Phoenix, in Drury–Lane. London: Printed by Nicholas Okes, for Richard Collins, and are to be sold at his shop, in St. Paul’s Church-yard, at the signe of the Three Kings, 1633.” It was one of the plays appropriated, by the Lord Chamberlain, to the Cockpit or Phoenix Theatre, in 1639.

This tragedy was selected for publication by Mr. Dodsley. The choice was not very judicious, for, though the language of it is eminently beautiful, the plot is repulsive: and the “Lover’s Melancholy,” or the “Broken Heart,” would have been fully as characteristic of the author’s manner. It owes little to the taste, and nothing to the judgment of the former editors. Dodsley merely copied the 4to. and Reed re-published the transcript with a few childish “Illustrations,” worth a sponge.

TO
THE TRULY NOBLE
JOHN,
EARL OF PETERBOROUGH, LORD MORDAUNT, BARON OF
TURVEY.

MY LORD,

Where a truth of merit hath a general warrant, there love is but a debt, acknowledgment a justice. Greatness cannot often claim virtue by inheritance; yet, in this, Your's appears most eminent, for that you are not more rightly heir to your fortunes than glory shall be to your memory. Sweetness of disposition ennobles a freedom of birth; in both, your lawful interest adds honour to your own name, and mercy to my presumption. Your noble allowance of these first fruits of my leisure, in the action, emboldens my confidence of your as noble construction in this presentment; especially since my service must ever owe particular duty to your favours, by a particular engagement.3 The gravity of the subject may easily excuse the lightness of the title, otherwise I had been a severe judge against mine own guilt. Princes have vouchsafed grace to trifles offered from a purity of devotion; your Lordship may likewise please to admit into your good opinion, with these weak endeavours, the constancy of affection from the sincere lover of your deserts in honour,

JOHN FORD.

      John, first Earl of Peterborough, Collins informs us, "obtained that dignity in the year 1627–8. He was brought up in the Romish religion, but was converted by a disputation at his own house, between the learned Bishop Usher (then only Dr. Usher) and a Papist, who confessed himself silenced by the just hand of God, for presuming to dispute without leave from his superiors." vol. iii. p. 317. No miraculous event appears to have confirmed his loyalty, (whatever may be said of his Jaith,) for "he joined the Parliamentary Army in 1642, and was made General of the Ordnance and Colonel of a regiment of foot, under Essex." His military career was of short duration; as "he departed this life June 18th the same year."

      So little of Ford's personal history is known, that no allusion to any circumstance peculiar to himself can be explained. He seems here (and all is but seeming) to speak of some legal business in which he was engaged under this nobleman; but of what nature, it would be useless to inquire.

Dramatis Personæ.

Bonaventura, a Friar.
A Cardinal, Nuncio to the Pope.
Soranzo, a Nobleman.
Florio, Donado, Citizens of Parma.
Grimaldi, a Roman Gentleman.
Giovanni, Son to Florio.
Bergetto, Nephew to Donado.
Richardetto, a supposed Physician.
Vasques, Servant to Soranzo.
Poggio, Servant to Bergetto.
Banditti.
Annabella, Daughter to Florio.
Hippolita, Wife to Richardetto.
Philotis, his Niece.
Putana, Tutoress to Annabella.
Officers, Attendants, Servants, etc.

The Scene — Parma.
ACT I.
SCENE I.

Friar Bonaventura's Cell.

Enter Friar and Giovanni.

Friar. Dispute no more in this; for know, young man,
    These are no school points; nice philosophy
    May tolerate unlikely arguments,
    But Heaven admits no jest: wits that presumed
    On wit too much, by striving how to prove
    There was no God, with foolish grounds of art,
    Discover'd first the nearest way to hell;
    And fill'd the world with devilish atheism.
    Such questions, youth, are fond[1]: far better 'tis[2]
    To bless the sun, than reason why it shines;
    Yet He thou talk'st of, is above the sun. —
    No more! I may not hear it.

Giovanni. Gentle father,
    To you I have unclasp'd my burden'd soul,
    Emptied the storehouse of my thoughts and heart,
    Made myself poor of secrets; have not left
    Another word untold, which hath not spoke
    All what I ever durst, or think, or know;
    And yet is here the comfort I shall have?
    Must I not do what all men else may — love?

Friar. Yes, you may love, fair son.

Giovanni. Must I not praise
    That beauty, which, if fram'd anew, the gods
    Would make a god of, if they had it there;
    And kneel to it, as I do kneel to them?

Friar. Why, foolish madman! —

Giovanni. Shall a peevish[3] sound,

---

[1] Fond. i. e. idle, unprofitable.
[2] Far better 'tis. The 4to. reads for. — Reed.

A customary form, from man to man,
Of brother and of sister, be a bar
'Twixt my perpetual happiness and me?
Say that we had one father, say one womb
(Curse to my joys!) gave both us-life and birth;
Are we not, therefore, each to other bound
So much the more by nature? by the links
Of blood, of reason? nay, if you will have it,
Even of religion, to be ever one,
One soul, one flesh, one love, one heart, one all?

Friar. Have done, unhappy youth! for thou art lost.

Giovanni. Shall, then, for that I am her brother born,
My joys be ever banished from her bed?
No, father; in your eyes I see the change
Of pity and compassion; from your age,
As from a sacred oracle, distils
The life of counsel: tell me, holy man,
What cure shall give me ease in these extremes?

Friar. Repentance, son, and sorrow for this sin:
For thou hast mov'd a Majesty above,
With thy unranged (almost) blasphemy.

Giovanni. O do not speak of that, dear confessor.

Friar. Art thou, my son, that miracle of wit,
Who once, within these three months, wert esteem'd
A wonder of thine age, throughout Bononia?
How did the University applaud
Thy government, behaviour, learning, speech,
Sweetness, and all that could make up a man!
I was proud of my tutelage, and chose
Rather to leave my books, than part with thee;
I did so:— but the fruits of all my hopes
Are lost in thee, as thou art in thy self.
O Giovanni![4] hast thou left the schools
Of knowledge, to converse with lust and death?

---

[3] Peevish. Weak, trifling, unimportant.
[4] O Giovanni! Our old dramatists appear to have learned Italian entirely from books; few, if any, of them pronounce it correctly. Giovanni is here used by Ford as a quadrisyllable, as it was by Massinger and others of his contemporaries.

For death waits on thy lust. Look through the world,
And thou shall see a thousand faces shine
More glorious than this idol thou ador'st:
Leave her, and take thy choice, 'tis much less sin;
Though in such games as those, they lose that win.

Giovanni. It were more ease to stop the ocean
From floats and ebbs, than to dissuade my vows.

Friar. Then I have done, and in thy wilful flames
Already see thy ruin; Heaven is just. —
Yet hear my counsel.

Giovanni. As a voice of life.

Friar. Hie to thy father's house, there lock thee fast
Alone within thy chamber; then fall down
On both thy knees, and grovel on the ground;
Cry to thy heart; wash every word thou utter'st
In tears (and if't be possible) of blood:
Beg Heaven to cleanse the leprosy of lust
That rots thy soul; acknowledge what thou art,
A wretch, a worm, a nothing; weep, sigh, pray
Three times a-day, and three times every night:
For seven days space do this; then, if thou find'st
No change in thy desires, return to me;
I'll think on remedy. Pray for thyself
At home, whilst I pray for thee here. — Away!
My blessing with thee! we have need to pray.

Giovanni. All this I'll do, to free me from the rod
Of vengeance; else I'll swear my fate's my god.

Exeunt[5].

---

[5] It is observed by Langbaine, that the loves of Giovanni and Annabella are painted in too beautiful colours: this, though it may impeach the writer's taste in selecting such a subject, is yet complimentary to his judgment in treating it. What but the most glowing diction, the most exquisite harmony of versification, could hope to allure the reader through the dreadful display of vice and misery which lay before him! With respect to the scene which has just past, it is replete with excellence as a composition; it may be doubted, however, whether it does not let us somewhat too abruptly into the plot, which, from its revolting nature, should have been more gradually opened. The character of the Friar is artfully drawn; pious, but gentle, irresolute, and, to speak tenderly, strangely indulgent; and thus we are prepared for his subsequent conduct, which involves the fate of his young charge.

SCENE II.

The Street, before Florio's House.

Enter Grimaldi and Vasques, with their Swords drawn.

Vasques. Come, sir, stand to your tackling; if you prove craven, I'll make you run quickly.

Grimaldi. Thou art no equal match for me.

Vasques. Indeed I never went to the wars to bring home news; nor I cannot play the mountebank for a meal's meat, and swear I got my wounds in the field. See you these grey hairs? they'll not flinch for a bloody nose. Wilt thou to this gear?

Grimaldi. Why, slave, think'st thou I'll balance my reputation with a cast-suit? Call thy master, he shall know that I dare —

Vasques. Scold like a cot-quean[6]; — that's your profession. Thou poor shadow of a soldier, I will make thee know my master keeps servants, thy betters in quality and performance. Com'st thou to fight or prate?

Grimaldi. Neither, with thee. I am a Roman and a gentleman; one that have got mine honour with expense of blood.

Vasques. You are a lying coward, and a fool. Fight, or by these hilts I'll kill thee:— brave my lord! You'll fight?

Grimaldi. Provoke me not, for if thou dost —

Vasques. Have at you.

They fight, Grimaldi is worsted.

Enter Florio, Donado, and Soranzo, from opposite Sides.

Florio. What mean these sudden broils so near my doors?
　　　　Have you not other places, but my house,
　　　　To vent the spleen of your disorder'd bloods?

---

[6] Scold like a cot-quean. A contemptuous term for one who concerns himself with female affairs; an effeminate meddler.

Must I be haunted still with such unrest,
As not to eat, or sleep in peace at home?
Is this your love, Grimaldi? Fie! 'tis naught.

Donado. And, Vasques, I may tell thee, 'tis not well
To broach these quarrels; you are ever forward
In seconding contentions.

Enter above[7] *Annabella and Putana.*

Florio. What's the ground?

Soranzo. That, with your patience, signiors, I'll resolve:
This gentleman, whom fame reports a soldier,
(For else I know not) rivals me in love
To Signior Florio's daughter; to whose ears
He still prefers his suit, to my disgrace;
Thinking the way to recommend himself,
Is to disparage me in his report. —
But know, Grimaldi, though, may be, thou art
My equal in thy blood, yet this bewrays
A lowness in thy mind; which, wert thou noble,
Thou would'st as much disdain, as I do thee
For this unworthiness; and on this ground
I will'd my servant to correct his tongue,
Holding a man so base no match for me.

Vasques. And had not your sudden coming prevented us, I had let my
gentleman blood under the gills; I should have worm'd you, sir, for
running mad[8].

Grimaldi. I'll be reveng'd, Soranzo.

Vasques. On a dish of warm broth to stay your stomach — do, honest
innocence, do! spoon-meat is a wholesomer diet than a Spanish
blade.

Grimaldi. Remember this! *Exit.*

---

[7] Enter above, i. e. on the raised platform which stood on the old stage, and which served for a balcony to the street, and a gallery to the rooms within doors.

[8] I should have worm'd you, sir, for running mad.] i. e. to prevent you from running mad. The allusion is, to the practice of cutting what is called the worm from under a dog's tongue, as a preventive of madness.

Soranzo. I fear thee not, Grimaldi.

Florio. My lord Soranzo, this is strange to me;
      Why you should storm, having my word engag'd:
      Owing her heart[9], what need you doubt her ear?
      Losers may talk, by law of any game.

Vasques. Yet the villainy of words, Signior Florio, may be such, as would
      make any unspleened dove choleric. Blame not my lord in this.

Florio. Be you more silent;
      I would not for my wealth, my daughter's love
      Should cause the spilling of one drop of blood.
      Vasques, put up: let's end this fray in wine.

Exeunt.

Putana. How like you this, child? here's threatening, challenging, quarrelling,
      and fighting on every side, and all is for your sake; you had need look
      to yourself, charge, you'll be stolen away sleeping else shortly.

Annabella. But, tutoress, such a life gives no content
      To me, my thoughts are fix'd on other ends.
      Would you would leave me!

Putana. Leave you! no marvel else; leave me no leaving, charge; this is love
      outright. Indeed, I blame you not; you have choice fit for the best
      lady in Italy.

Annabella. Pray do not talk so much.

Putana. Take the worst with the best, there's Grimaldi the soldier, a very well
      tiinber'd fellow. They say he's a Roman, nephew to the Duke
      Montferrato; they say he did good service in the wars against the
      Milanese; but, 'faith, charge, I do not like him, an't be for nothing but
      for being a soldier: not one amongst twenty of your skirmishing
      captains but have some privy maim or other, that mars their standing

---

[9] Owing her heart, i. e. possessing, oicning: in this sense the word is used by all our old dramatists. Florio's reasoning, however, is far from correct. It does not follow that, because Soranzo had his word, be owed his daughter's heart: in short, Annabella seems to have thought nothing of him.

upright. I like him the worse, he crinkles so much in the hams: though he might serve if there were no more men, yet he's not the man I would choose.

Annabella. Fie, how thou prat'st!

Putana. As I am a very woman, I like Signior So — ranzo well; he is wise, and what is more, rich; and what is more than that, kind; and what is more than all this, a nobleman: such a one, were I the fair Annabella myself, I would wish and pray for. Then he is bountiful; besides, he is handsome, and by my troth, I think, wholesome; and that's news in a gallant of three-and-twenty: liberal, that I know; loving, that you know; and a man sure, else he could never have purchased such a good name with Hippolita, the lusty widow, in her husband's lifetime. An 'twere but for that report, sweetheart, would he were thine! Commend a man for his qualities, but take a husband as he is a plain, sufficient, naked man; such a one is for your bed, and such a one is Signior Soranzo, my life for't.

Annabella. Sure the woman took her morning's draught too soon.

Enter Bergetto and Poggio.

Putana. But look, sweetheart, look what thing comes now! Here's another of your ciphers to fill up the number: Oh, brave old ape in a silken coat! Observe.

Bergetto. Didst thou think, Poggio, that I would spoil my new clothes, and leave my dinner, to fight!

Poggio. No, sir, I did not take you for so arrant a baby.

Bergetto. I am wiser than so: for I hope, Poggio, thou never heardst of an elder brother that was a coxcomb; didst, Poggio?

Poggio. Never indeed, sir, as long as they had either land or money left them to inherit.

Bergetto. Is it possible, Poggio? Oh, monstrous! Why, I'll undertake, with a handful of silver, to buy a headful of wit at any time: but, sirrah, I have another purchase in hand; I shall have the wench, mine uncle says. I will but wash my face, and shift socks; and then have at her, i'faith. — Mark my pace, Poggio! *Passes over the Stage.*

Poggio. Sir — I have seen an ass and a mule trot the Spanish pavin[10] with a better grace, I know not how often. [Aside, and following him.

Annabella. This idiot haunts me too.

Putana. Ay, ay, he needs no description. The rich magnifico that is below with your father, charge, Signior Donado his uncle, for that he means to make this, his cousin, a golden calf, thinks that you will be a right Israelite, and fall down to him presently: but I hope I have tutored you better. They say a fool's bauble is a lady's play-fellow; yet you, having wealth enough, you need not cast upon the dearth of flesh, at any rate. Hang him, innocent![11]
Giovanni passes over the Stage.

Annabella. But see, Putana, see! what blessed shape
Of some celestial creature now appears! —
What man is he, that with such sad aspect
Walks careless of himself?

Putana. Where?

Annabella. Look below.

Putana. Oh, 'tis your brother, sweet.

Annabella. Ha!

Putana. Tis your brother.

Annabella. Sure 'tis not he; this is some woeful thing
Wrapp'd up in grief, some shadow of a man.
Alas! he beats his breast, and wipes his eyes,
Drown'd all in tears: methinks I hear him sigh;

---

[10] The Spanish pavin. "The Pavan, from Pavo, a peacock, is a grave and majestic dance; the method of performing it was anciently by gentlemen, dressed with a cap and sword; by those of the long robe, in their gowns; by princes, in their mantles, and by ladies, in gowns with long trains, the motion whereof in the dance resembled that of a peacock's tail."— Sir John Hawkins.

[11] Innocent. A natural fool. Thus, in the Two Noble Kinsmen, A. iv. s. 4. "but this very day I ask'd her questions, and she answer'd roe So far from what she was, so childishly, So sillily, as if she were a fool, An innocent; and I was very angry."— Reed.

Let's down, Putana, and partake the cause.
I know my brother, in the love he bears me,
Will not deny me partage in his sadness:
My soul is full of heaviness and fear.

Aside, and exit with Put.

SCENE III.

A Hall in Florio's House.

Giovanni. Lost! I am lost! my fates have doom'd my death:
      The more I strive, I love; the more I love,
      The less I hope: I see my ruin certain.
      What judgment or endeavours could apply
      To my incurable and restless wounds,
      I thoroughly have examined, but in vain.
      O, that it were not in religion sin
      To make our love a god, and worship it!
      I have even wearied heaven with pray'rs, dried up
      The spring of my continual tears, even starv'd
      My veins with daily fasts: what wit or art
      Could counsel, I have practised; but, alas!
      I find all these but dreams, and old men's tales,
      To fright unsteady youth; I am still the same:
      Or I must speak, or burst. Tis not, I know,
      My lust, but 'tis my fate, that leads me on[12].
      Keep fear and low faint-hearted shame with slaves!
      I'll tell her that I love her, though my heart
      Were rated at the price of that attempt.
      Oh me! she comes.

Enter Annabella and Putana.

Annabella. Brother!

Giovanni. If such a thing
      As courage dwell in men, ye heavenly powers,
      Now double all that virtue in my tongue! [Aside.

Annabella. Why, brother,
      Will you not speak to me?

Giovanni. Yes; how do you, sister?

---

[12] This is a repetition of the sentiment with which he had taken leave of the Friar — My fate's my god. I would not detain the reader in these scenes, on which Ford has lavished all the charms of bis eloquence; but it may be cursorily observed, that characters like Giovanni, desperately abandoned to vice, endeavour to cheat their conscience, by setting up a deity of their own, and pretending to be swayed by his resistless influence. This is the last stage of human depravation, and, in Scripture language, is called "hardening the heart."

Annabella. Howe'er I am, methinks you are not well.

Putana. Bless us! why are you so sad, sir?

Giovanni. Let me entreat you, leave us a while,

Putana. Sister, I would be private with you.

Annabella. Withdraw, Putana.

Putana. I will. — If this were any other company for her, I should think my
    absence an office of some credit; but I will leave them together.
Aside, and exit.

Giovanni. Come, sister, lend your hand; let's walk together;
I hope you need not blush to walk with me;
Here's none but you and I.

Annabella. How's this?

Giovanni. I'faith,
    I mean no harm.

Annabella. Harm?

Giovanni. No, good faith. How is it with thee?

Annabella. I trust he be not frantic — [Aside.
    I am very well, brother.

Giovanni. Trust me, but I am sick; I fear so sick,
    'Twill cost my life.

Annabella. Mercy forbid it! 'tis not so, I hope.

Giovanni. I think you love me, sister.

Annabella. Yes, you know I do.

Giovanni. I know it, indeed — you are very fair.

Annabella. Nay, then I see you have a merry sickness.

Giovanni. That's as it proves. The poets feign, I read,
     That Juno for her forehead did exceed
     All other goddesses; but I durst swear
     Your forehead exceeds her's, as her's did theirs.

Annabella. Troth, this is pretty!

Giovanni. Such a pair of stars
     As are thine eyes, would, like Promethean fire,
     If gently glanced, give life to senseless stones.

Annabella. Fie upon you!

Giovanni. The lily and the rose, most sweetly strange,
     Upon your dimple cheeks do strive for change:
     Such lips would tempt a saint; such hands as those
     Would make an anchorite lascivious.

Annabella. Do you mock me, or flatter me?

Giovanni. If you would see a beauty more exact
     Than art can counterfeit, or nature frame,
     Look in your glass, and there behold your own.

Annabella. O, you are a trim youth!

Giovanni. Here! [Offers his dagger to her.

Annabella. What to do?

Giovanni. And here's my breast; strike home!
     Rip up my bosom, there thou shalt behold
     A heart, in which is writ the truth I speak —
     Why stand you?

Annabella. Are you earnest?

Giovanni. Yes, most earnest. You cannot love?

Annabella. Whom?

Giovanni. Me. My tortured soul

Hath felt affliction in the heat of death.
O, Annabella, I am quite undone!
The love of thee, my sister, and the view
Of thy immortal beauty, have untuned
All harmony both of my rest and life.
Why do you not strike?

Annabella. Forbid it, my just fears!
If this be true, 'twere fitter I were dead.

Giovanni. True! Annabella; 'tis no time to jest.
I have too long suppress'd my hidden flames,
That almost have consum'd me; I have spent
Many a silent night in sighs and groans;
Ran over all my thoughts, despised my fate,
Reason'd against the reasons of my love,
Done all that smooth-cheek'd virtue could advise,
But found all bootless: 'tis my destiny
That you must either love, or I must die.

Annabella. Comes this in sadness[13] from you?

Giovanni. Let some mischief
Befall me soon, if I dissemble aught.

Annabella. You are my brother Giovanni.

Giovanni. You
My sister Annabella; I know this,
And could afford you instance why to love
So much the more for this; to which intent
Wise nature first in your creation meant
To make you mine; else't had been sin and foul
To share one beauty to a double soul.
Nearness in birth and blood, doth but persuade
A nearer nearness in affection.
I have ask'd counsel of the holy church,
Who tells me I may love you; and, 'tis just,
That, since I may, I should; and will, yes will:
Must I now live, or die?

---

[13] Comes this in sadness. i. e. in seriousness.

Annabella. Live; thou hast won
       The field, and never fought: what thou hast urged,
       My captive heart had long ago resolv'd.
       I blush to tell thee — but I'll tell thee now —
       For every sigh that thou hast spent for me,
       I have sigh'd ten; for every tear, shed twenty:
       And not so much for that I loved, as that
       I durst not say I loved, nor scarcely think it.

Giovanni. Let not this music be a dream, ye gods,
       For pity's sake, I beg you!

Annabella. On my knees, [*She kneels.*
       Brother, even by our mother's dust, I charge you,
       Do not betray me to your mirth or hate;
       Love me, or kill me, brother.

Giovanni. On my knees, [*He kneels.*
       Sister, even by my mother's dust I charge you,
       Do not betray me to your mirth or hate;
       Love me, or kill me, sister.

Annabella. You mean good sooth, then?

Giovanni. In good troth, I do;
       And so do you, I hope: say, I'm in earnest.

Annabella. I'll swear it, I[14].

Giovanni. And I; and by this kiss. *Kisses her.*
       (Once more, yet once more; now let's rise) *they rise*
       by this, I would not change this minute for Elysium.
       What must we now do?

Annabella. What you will.

Giovanni. Come then;
       After so many tears as we have wept,
       Let's learn to court in smiles, to kiss, and sleep. *Exeunt.*

---

[14] Til swear it, I. The old copy has and before I; evidently an oversight of the press.

SCENE IV.

A Street.

Enter Florio and Donado.

Florio. Signior Donado, you have said enough,
     I understand you; but would have you know,
     I will not force my daughter 'gainst her will.
     You see I have but two, a son and her;
     And he is so devoted to his book,
     As I must tell you true, I doubt his health:
     Should he miscarry, all my hopes rely
     Upon my girl[15]. As for worldly fortune,
     I am, I thank my stars, bless'd with enough.
     My care is, how to match her to her liking;
     I would not have her marry wealth, but love,
     And if she like your nephew, let him have her;
     Here's all that I can say.

Donado. Sir, you say well,
     Like a true father; and, for my part, I,
     If the young folks can like, ('twixt you and me)
     Will promise to assure my nephew presently
     Three thousand florins yearly, during life,
     And, after I am dead, my whole estate.

Florio. Tis a fair proffer, sir; meantime your nephew
     Shall have free passage to commence his suit:
     If he can thrive, he shall have my consent;
     So for this time I'll leave you, signior. [Exit.

Donado. Well,
     Here's hope yet, if my nephew would have wit;
     But he is such another dunce, I fear
     He'll never win the wench. When I was young,
     I could have don't, i'faith, and so shall he,
     If he will learn of me; and, in good time,
     He comes himself.

---

[15] Upon my girl. Girl is here, and almost every where else in these plays, a dissyllable. The practice is not peculiar to our poet, for Fanshaw, and others of that age, have numerous examples of it.

Enter Bergetto and Poggio.

      How now, Bergetto, whither away so fast?

Bergetto. Oh uncle! I have heard the strangest news that ever came out of the mint; have I not, Poggio?

Poggio. Yes, indeed, sir.

Donado. What news, Bergetto?

Bergetto. Why, look ye, uncle, my barber told me just now, that there is a fellow come to town, who undertakes to make a mill go without the mortal help of any water or wind, only with sandbags; and this fellow hath a strange horse, a most excellent beast, I'll assure you, uncle, my barber says; whose head, to the wonder of all Christian people, stands just behind where his tail is. Is't not true, Poggio?

Poggio. So the barber swore, forsooth.

Donado. And you are running thither?

Bergetto. Ay, forsooth, uncle.

Donado. Wilt thou be a fool still? Come, sir, you shall not go; you have more mind of a puppet-play than on the business I told you: why, thou great baby, wilt never have wit? wilt make thyself a May-game to all the world?

Poggio. Answer for yourself, master.

Bergetto. Why, uncle, should I sit at home still, and not go abroad to see fashions like other gallants?

Donado. To see hobby-horses! what wise talk, I pray, had you with Annabella, when you were at Signior Florio's house?

Bergetto. Oh, the wench! — Uds sa'me, uncle, I tickled her with a rare speech, that I made her almost burst her belly with laughing.

Donado. Nay, I think so; and what speech was't?

Bergetto. What did I say, Poggio?

Poggio. Forsooth, my master said, that he loved her almost as well as he loved parmasent[16]; and swore (I'll be sworn for him) that she wanted but such a nose as his was, to be as pretty a young woman as any was in Parma.

Donado. Oh gross!

Bergetto. Nay, uncle; — then she ask'd me, whether my father had more children than myself? and I said no; 'twere better he should have had his brains knock'd out first.

Donado. This is intolerable.

Bergetto. Then said she, will Signior Donado, your uncle, leave you all his wealth?

Donado. Ha! that was good; did she harp upon that string?

Bergetto. Did she harp upon that string! ay, that she did. I answer'd, "Leave me all his wealth? why, woman, he hath no other wit; if he had, he should hear on't to his everlasting glory and confusion: I know, quoth I, I am his white boy[17], and will not be gull'd;" and with that she fell into a great smile, and went away. Nay, I did fit her.

Donado. Ah, sirrah, then I see there's no changing of nature. Well, Bergetto, I fear thou wilt be a very ass still.

Bergetto. I should be sorry for that, uncle.

Donado. Come, come you home with me: since you are no better a speaker, I'll have you write to her after some courtly manner, and enclose some rich jewel in the letter.

Bergetto. Ay marry, that will be excellent.

Donado. Peace, innocent!
Once in my time I'll set my wits to school,

---

[16] Parmasent. i. e. Parmasan; the cheese of Parma, where the scene is laid. — Reed suggests that this word may mean a trick in drinking so Called; but poor Bergetto had no tricks of any kind: the allusion is evidently to the cheese, which is sufficiently strong to affect the breath, and therefore ridiculously put in competition with the lady.

[17] White-boy. A childish term of endearment. Warton says that Dr. Busby used to call his favourite scholars his white-boys. The word occurs in Massinger, and most of pur old poets.

If all fail, 'tis but the fortune of a fool.

Bergetto. Poggio, 'twill do, Poggio!

Exeunt.

ACT II.
SCENE I.

An Apartment in Florio's House.

Enter Giovanni and Annabella.

Giovanni. Come, Annabella, no more Sister now,
      But Love, a name more gracious; do not blush,
      Beauty's sweet wonder, but be proud to know
      That yielding thou hast conquer'd, and inflamed
      A heart, whose tribute is thy brother's life.

Annabella. And mine is his. Oh, how these stolen contents
      Would print a modest crimson on my cheeks,
      Had any but my heart's delight prevail'd!

Giovanni. I marvel why the chaster of your sex
      Should think this pretty toy call'd maidenhead,
      So strange a loss; when, being lost, 'tis nothing,
      And you are still the same.

Annabella. Tis well for you;
      Now you can talk.

Giovanni. Music as well consists
      In th' ear, as in the playing.

Annabella. Oh, you are wanton! —
      Tell on't, you were best; do.

Giovanni. Thou wilt chide me then.
      Kiss me — so! thus hung Jove on Leda's neck,
      And suck'd divine ambrosia from her lips.
      I envy not the mightiest man alive;
      But hold myself, in being king of thee,
      More great than were I king of all the world:
      But I shall lose you, sweetheart.

Annabella. But you shall not.

Giovanni. You must be married, mistress.

Annabella. Yes! to whom?

Giovanni. Some one must have you.

Annabella. You must.

Giovanni. Nay, some other.

Annabella. Now prithee do not speak so; without jesting
      You'll make me weep in earnest.

Giovanni. What, you will not!
      But tell me, sweet, canst thou be dared to swear
      That thou wilt live to me, and to no other?

Annabella. By both our loves I dare; for didst thou know,
      My Giovanni, how all suitors seem
      To my eyes hateful, thou would'st trust me then.

Giovanni. Enough, I take thy word: sweet, we must part;
Remember what thou vow'st; keep well my heart.

Annabella. Will you be gone?

Giovanni. I must.

Annabella. When to return?

Giovanni. Soon.

Annabella. Look you do.

Giovanni. Farewell. *Exit.*

Annabella. Go where thou wilt, in mind I'll keep thee here,
      And where thou art, I know I shall be there.
      Guardian!

Enter Putana.

Putana. Child, how is't, child? well, thank heav'n, ha?

Annabella. O guardian, what a paradise of joy Have I past over!

Putana. Nay, what a paradise of joy have you past under! why, now I commend thee, charge. Fear nothing, sweet-heart; what though he be your brother? your brother's a man, I hope; and I say still, if a young wench feel the fit upon her, let her take any body, father or brother, all is one.

Annabella. I would not have it known for all the world.

Putana. Nor I indeed; for the speech of the people; else 'twere nothing.

Florio. (within) Daughter Annabella!

Annabella. O me! my father, Here, sir:— reach my work.

Florio. (within) What are you doing?

Annabella. So; let him come now.

Enter Florio, followed by Richardetto as a Doctor of Physic, and Philotis, with a Lute.

Florio. So hard at work! that's well; you lose no time.
　　　　Look, I have brought you company; here's one,
　　　　A learned doctor, lately come from Padua,
　　　　Much skill'd in physic; and, for that I see
　　　　You have of late been sickly, I entreated
　　　　This reverend man to visit you some time.

Annabella. You are very welcome, sir.

Richardetto. I thank you, mistress:
Loud fame in large report hath spoke your praise,
As well for virtue as perfection[18];
For which I have been bold to bring with me
A kinswoman of mine, a maid, for song
And music, one perhaps will give content;
Please you to know her.

Annabella. They are parts I love,
And she for them most welcome.

---

[18] As well for virtue as perfection. For perfect beauty, or fullness of accomplishments.

Philotis. Thank you, lady.

Florio. Sir, now you know my house, pray make not strange;
   And if you find my daughter need your art,
   I'll be your pay-master.

Richardetto. Sir, what I am
   She shall command.

Florio. You shall bind me to you.
   Daughter, I must have conference with you
   About some matters that concern us both.
   Good master doctor, please you but walk in,
   We'll crave a little of your cousin's cunning[19];
   I think my girl hath not quite forgot
   To touch an instrument; she could have don't;
   We'll hear them both.

Richardetto. I'll wait upon you, sir.

Exeunt.

---

[19] Cunning. i. e skill in music: the word is used in this sense by all our old writers.

SCENE II.

A Room in Soranzo's House.

Enter Soranzo, with a Book.

Loves measure is extreme, the comfort pain;
The life unrest, and the reward disdain.

What's here? look't o'er again. — 'Tis so; so writes
This smooth licentious poet in his rhymes:
But, Sannazar, thou ly'st; for, had thy bosom
Felt such oppression as is laid on mine,
Thou would'st have kiss'd the rod that made the[e] smart.
To work then, happy muse, and contradict
What Sannazar hath in his envy writ. *Writes.*

Loves measure is the mean, sweet his annoys;
His pleasures life, and his reward all joys.

Had Annabella liv'd when Sannazar
Did, in his brief Encomium[20], celebrate
Venice, that queen of cities, he had left
That verse which gain'd him such a sum of gold,
And for one only look from Annabel,
Had writ of her, and her diviner cheeks.
O, how my thoughts are —

Vasques. (within) Pray forbear; in rules of civility, let me give notice on't: I
shall be tax'd of my neglect of duty and service.

Soranzo. What rude intrusion interrupts my peace?

---

[20] when Sannazar did in his brief Encomium, etc. This is the well known Epigram, beginning "Viderat Hadriacis Venetam Neptunus in undis stare urbem," etc.

It is given by Coryat, who thus speaks of it: "I heard in Venice that a certaine Italian poet, called Jacobus Sannazarius, had a hundred crownes bestowed upon him by the Senate of Venice for each of these verses following. I would to God my poetical friend Master Benjamin Johnson were so well rewarded for his poems here in England, seeing he hath made many as good verses (in my opinion) as those of Sannazarius." Tom is right. The verses have nothing very extraordinary in them; but they flattered the vanity of the republic: and after all, there is no great evil in overpaying a poet once in fifteen centuries, for so long it is between the times of Virgil and Sannazarius.

Can I be no where private?

Vasques. (within) Troth, you wrong your modesty.

Soranzo. What's the matter, Vasques? who is't?

Enter Hippolita and Vasques.

Hippolita. Tis I;
      Do you know me now? Look, perjur'd man, on her
      Whom thou and thy distracted lust have wrong'd.
      Thy sensual rage of blood hath made my youth
      A scorn to men and angels; and shall I
      Be now a foil to thy unsated change?
      Thou know'st, false wanton, when my modest fame
      Stood free from stain or scandal, all the charms
      Of hell or sorcery could not prevail
      Against the honour of my chaster bosom.
      Thine eyes did plead in tears, thy tongue in oaths,
      Such, and so many, that a heart of steel
      Would have been wrought to pity, as was mine;
      And shall the conquest of my lawful bed,
      My husband's death, urg'd on by his disgrace,
      My loss of womanhood, be ill-rewarded
      With hatred and contempt? No; know, Soranzo,
      I have a spirit doth as much distaste
      The slavery of fearing thee, as thou
      Dost loath the memory of what hath past.

Soranzo. Nay, dear Hippolita —

Hippolita. Call me not dear,
      Nor think with supple words to smooth the grossness
      Of my abuses; 'tis not your new mistress,
      Your goodly madam-merchant, shall triumph
      On my dejection; tell her thus from me,
      My birth was nobler, and by much more free.

Soranzo. You are too violent.

Hippolita. You are too double
      In your dissimulation. Seest thou this,
      This habit, these black mourning weeds of care?

Tis thou art cause of this; and hast divorced
My husband from his life, and me from him,
And made me widow in my widowhood.

Soranzo. Will you yet hear?

Hippolita. More of thy perjuries?
    Thy soul is drown'd too deeply in those sins;
    Thou need'st not add to th' number.

Soranzo. Then I'll leave you;
    You are past all rules of sense.

Hippolita. And thou of grace.

Vasques. Fie, mistress, you are not near the limits of reason; if my lord had a
    resolution as noble as virtue itself, you take the course to unedge it
    all. Sir, I beseech you do not perplex her; griefs, alas, will have a vent:
    I dare undertake madam Hippolita will now freely hear you.

Soranzo. Talk to a woman frantic! — Are these the fruits of your love?

Hippolita. They are the fruits of thy untruth, false man!
    Did'st thou not swear, whilst yet my husband liv'd.
    That thou would'st wish no happiness on earth
    More than to call me wife? didst thou not vow,
    When he should die, to marry me? for which
    The devil in my blood, and thy protests,
    Caus'd me to counsel him to undertake
    A voyage to Ligorne, for that we heard
    His brother there was dead, and left a daughter
    Young and unfriended, whom, with much ado,
    I wish'd him to bring hither: he did so,
    And went; and, as thou know'st, died on the way.
    Unhappy man, to buy his death so dear,
    With my advice! yet thou, for whom I did it,
    Forget'st thy vows, and leav'st me to my shame.

Soranzo. Who could help this?

Hippolita. Who? perjur'd man! thou could'st,
    If thou had'st faith or love.

Soranzo. You are deceiv'd;
     The vows I made, if you remember well,
     Were wicked and unlawful; 'twere more sin
     To keep them than to break them: as for me,
     I cannot mask my penitence. Think thou
     How much thou hast digress'd from honest shame,
     In bringing of a gentleman to death,
     Who was thy husband; such a one as he,
     So noble in his quality, condition,
     Learning, behaviour, entertainment, love,
     As Parma could not show a braver man.

Vasques. You do not well; this was not your promise.

Soranzo. I care not; let her know her monstrous life.
     Ere I'll be servile to so black a sin,
     I'll be a curse. —— Woman, come here no more;
     Learn to repent, and die; for, by my honour,
     I hate thee and thy lust: you have been too foul,
Exit.

Vasques. This part has been scurvily play'd. [Aside.

Hippolita. How foolishly this beast contemns his fate,
     And shuns the use of that, which I more scorn
     Than I once lov'd, his love! but let him go,
     My vengeance shall give comfort to his woe[21].
Going.

Vasques. Mistress, mistress, madam Hippolita! pray, a word or two.

Hippolita. With me, sir?

Vasques. With you, if you please.

Hippolita. Whatis't?

---

[21] To his woe. i. e. to the woe occasioned by his falsehood. She recurs to this idea in the concluding speech of this scene.

Vasques. I know you are infinitely moved now, and you think you have cause; some I confess you have, but sure not so much as you imagine.

Hippolita. Indeed!

Vasques. O you were miserably bitter, which you followed even to the last syllable; 'faith, you were somewhat too shrewd: by my life, you could not have took my lord in a worse time since I first knew him; tomorrow, you shall find him a new man.

Hippolita. Well, I shall wait his leisure.

Vasques. Fie, this is not a hearty patience; it comes sourly from you; 'troth, let me persuade you for once.

Hippolita. I have it, and it shall be so; thanks opportunity — *Aside.* — Persuade me! to what?

Vasques. Visit him in some milder temper. O, if you could but master a little your female spleen, how might you win him!

Hippolita. He will never love me. Vasques, thou hast been a too trusty servant to such a master, and I believe thy reward in the end will fall out like mine.

Vasques. So perhaps too.

Hippolita. Resolve[22] thyself it will. Had I one so true, so truly honest, so secret to my counsels, as thou hast been to him and his, I should think it a slight acquittance, not only to make him master of all I have, but even of myself.

Vasques. O you are a noble gentlewoman!

Hippolita. Wilt thou feed always upon hopes? well, I know thou art wise, and seest the reward of an old servant daily, what it is.

Vasques. Beggary and neglect.

---

[22] Resolve thyself it will. i. e. assure, convince thyself. The word occurs just below in the same sense.

Hippolita. True; but, Vasques, wert thou mine, and would'st be private to
      me and my designs, I here protest, myself, and all what I can else call
      mine, should be at thy dispose.

Vasques. Work you that way, old mole? then I have the wind of you —
      Aside. — I were not worthy of it by any desert that could lie within
      my compass; if I could —

Hippolita. What then?

Vasques. I should then hope to live in these my old years with rest and
      security.

Hippolita. Give me thy hand: now promise but thy silence,
      And help to bring to pass a plot I have;
      And here, in sight of Heaven, that being done,
      I make thee lord of me and mine estate.

Vasques. Come, you are merry; this is such a happiness that I can neither
      think or believe.

Hippolita. Promise thy secrecy, and 'tis confirm'd.

Vasques. Then here I call our good genii for witnesses, whatsoever your
      designs are, or against whomsoever, I will not only be a special actor
      therein, but never disclose it till it be effected.

Hippolita. I take thy word, and, with that, thee for mine;
      Come then, let's more confer of this anon. —
      On this delicious bane my thought shall banquet,
      Revenge shall sweeten what my griefs have tasted.

Aside, and exit with Vasques.

SCENE III.

The Street.

Enter Richardetto and Philotis.

Richardetto. Thou seest, my lovely niece, these strange mishaps,
　　　How all my fortunes turn to my disgrace;
　　　Wherein I am but as a looker-on,
　　　Whilst others act my shame, and I am silent.

Philotis. But, uncle, wherein can this borrow'd shape
　　　Give you content?

Richardetto. I'll tell thee, gentle niece:
　　　Thy wanton aunt in her lascivious riots
　　　Lives now secure, thinks I am surely dead,
　　　In my late journey to Ligorne for you;
　　　As I have caus'd it to be rumour'd out.
　　　Now would I see with what an impudence
　　　She gives scope to her loose adultery,
　　　　　And how the common voice allows hereof;
　　　Thus far I have prevail'd.

Philotis. Alas, I fear
　　　You mean some strange revenge.

Richardetto. O be not troubled,
　　　Your ignorance shall plead for you in all —
　　　But to our business. — What! you learn'd for certain,
　　　How Signior Florio means to give his daughter
　　　In marriage to Soranzo?

Philotis. Yes, for certain.

Richardetto. But how find you young Annabella's love
　　　Inclined to him?

Philotis. For aught I could perceive,
　　　She neither fancies him or any else.

Richardetto. There's mystery in that, which time must shew.
　　　She us'd you kindly?

Philotis. Yes.

Richardetto. And crav'd your company?

Philotis. Often.

Richardetto. Tis well; it goes as I could wish.
       I am the doctor now, and as for you,
       None knows you; if all fail not, we shall thrive.
       But who comes here? — I know him; 'tis Grimaldi,
       A Roman and a soldier, near allied
       Unto the Duke of Montferrato, one
       Attending on the nuncio of the pope
       That now resides in Parma; by which means
       He hopes to get the love of Annabella.

Enter Grimaldi.

Grimaldi. Save you, sir.

Richardetto. And you, sir.

Grimaldi. I have heard
       Of your approved skill, which through the city
       Is freely talk'd of, and would crave your aid.

Richardetto. For what, sir?

Grimaldi. Marry, sir, for this
       But I would speak in private.

Richardetto. Leave us, cousin. [Phi. retires.

Grimaldi. I love fair Annabella, and would know
Whether in arts there may not be receipts
To move affection.

Richardetto. Sir, perhaps there may;
But these will nothing profit you.

Grimaldi. Not me?

Richardetto. Unless I be mistook, you are a man

Greatly in favour with the cardinal.

Grimaldi. What of that?

Richardetto. In duty to his grace,
      I will be bold to tell you, if you seek
      To marry Florio's daughter, you must first
      Remove a bar 'twixt you and her.

Grimaldi. Who's that?

Richardetto. Soranzo is the man that hath her heart,
      And while he lives, be sure you cannot speed.

Grimaldi. Soranzo! what, mine enemy[23]? is it he?

Richardetto. Is he your enemy?

Grimaldi. The man I hate
      Worse than confusion; I will tell him straight. —

Richardetto. Nay, then take my advice,
      Even for his grace's sake the cardinal;
      I'll find a time when he and she do meet,
      Of which I'll give you notice; and, to be sure
      He shall not scape you, I'll provide a poison
      To dip your rapier's point in; if he had
      As many heads as Hydra had, he dies.

Grimaldi. But shall I trust thee, doctor?

Richardetto. As yourself;
      Doubt not in aught. —[*Exit Grim.*]— Thus shall the fates decree,
      By me Soranzo falls, that ruin'd me[24].

Exeunt.

---

[23] Grim. Soranzo! what, mine enemy? It is strange that this should appear a new discovery to Grimaldi, when he had been fully apprized of it in the rencontre with Vasques in the first act. It is not often, however, that Ford thus wholly forgets himself. In the next line there is apparently some slight error: "I'll tell hhn straight," should probably be, "I'll to him straight."

[24] that ruin'd me. The old copy reads — "that min'd me." What a detestable set of characters has Ford here sharked up for the exercise of his fine talents! With the exception of poor Bergetto and his uncle, most of the rest seem contending which of them shall prove worthiest of the wheel and the gibbet.

SCENE IV.

Another Part of the Street.

Enter Donado, with a Letter, Bergetto, and Poggio.

Donado. Well, sir, I must be content to be both your secretary and your messenger myself. I cannot tell what this letter may work; but, as sure as I am alive, if thou come once to talk with her, I fear thou wilt mar whatsoever I make.

Bergetto. You make, uncle! why am not I big enough to carry mine own letter, I pray?

Donado. Ay, ay, carry a fool's head of thy own! why, thou dunce, would'st thou write a letter, and carry it thyself?

Bergetto. Yes, that I would, and read it to her with mine own mouth; for you must think, if she will not believe me myself when she hears me speak, she will not believe another's hand-writing. Oh, you think I am a blockhead, uncle. No, sir, Poggio knows I have indited a letter myself; so I have.

Poggio. Yes truly, sir, I have it in my pocket.

Donado. A sweet one, no doubt; pray let's see it.

Bergetto. I cannot read my own hand very well, Poggio; read it, Poggio.

Donado. Begin.

Poggio. [*reads*] Most dainty and honey-sweet mistress, I could call you fair, and lie as fast as any that loves you; but my uncle being the elder man, I leave it to him, as more fit for his age, and the colour of his beard. I am wise enough to tell you I can bourd[25] where I see occasion; or if you like my uncle's wit better than mine, you shall marry me; if you like mine better than his, I will marry you, in spite of your teeth. So commending my best parts to you, I rest
Yours, upwards and downwards, or you may choose. Bergetto.

---

[25] I can bourd where I see occasion, i. e. jest. In the old spelling, this word is frequently confounded with board, which, as Sir Toby truly says, meant to accost. The words in the text are borrowed from Nic. Bottom, confessedly a very facetious personage.

Bergetto. Ah, ha! here's stuff, uncle!

Donado. Here's stuff indeed — to shame us all. Pray whose advice did you take in this learned letter?

Poggio. None, upon my word, but mine own.

Bergetto. And mine, uncle, believe it, nobody's else; 'twas mine own brain, I thank a good wit for't.

Donado. Get you home, sir, and look you keep within doors till I return.

Bergetto. How? that were a jest indeed! I scorn it, i'faith.

Donado. What! you do not?

Bergetto. Judge me, but I do now.

Poggio. Indeed, sir, 'tis very unhealthy.

Donado. Well, sir, if I hear any of your apish running to motions[26] and fopperies, till I come back, you were as good not; look to't.
Exit.

Bergetto. Poggio, shall's steal to see this horse with the head in's tail?

Poggio. Ay, but you must take heed of whipping.

Bergetto. Dost take me for a child, Poggio? Come, honest Poggio.

Exeunt.

---

[26] If I hear of your running to motions. i. e. to puppet-shews

SCENE V.

Friar Bonaventura's Cell.

Enter Friar and Giovanni.

Friar. Peace! thou hast told a tale, whose every word
      Threatens eternal slaughter to the soul;
      I'm sorry I have heard it: would mine ears
      Had been one minute deaf, before the hour
      That thou cam'st to me! O young man, cast-away,
      By the religious number of mine order[27],
      I day and night have wak'd my aged eyes
      Above my strength, to weep on thy behalf:
      But Heaven is angry, and be thou resolv'd,
      Thou art a man remark'd to taste a mischief[28].
      Look for't; though it come late, it will come sure.

Giovanni. Father, in this you are uncharitable;
      What I have done, I'll prove both fit and good.
      It is a principle which you have taught,
      When I was yet your scholar, that the frame
      And composition of the mind doth follow
      The frame and composition of [the] body:
      So, where the body's furniture is beauty,
      The mind's must needs be virtue; which aliow'd,
      Virtue itself is reason but refined,
      And love the quintessence of that: this proves
      My sister's beauty, being rarely fair,
      Is rarely virtuous; chiefly in her love,
      And chiefly, in that love, her love to me:
      If her's to me, then so is mine to her;
      Since in like causes are effects alike.

Friar. O ignorance in knowledge! long ago,
      How often have I warn'd thee this before?
      Indeed, if we were sure there were no Deity,
      Nor heaven nor hell; then to be led alone
      By nature's light (as were philosophers
      Of elder times) might instance some defence.

---

[27] By the religious number of mine order. A misprint, probably, for founder; but I have changed nothing.
[28] Thou art a man remark'd to taste a mischief. i. e. marked out to experience some fearful evil: in this seuse the word mischief is sometimes used by our old writers.

But 'tis not so: then, madman, thou wilt find,
That nature is in Heaven's positions blind.

Giovanni. Your age o'errules you; had you youth like mine,
You'd make her love your heaven, and her divine.

Friar. Nay, then I see thou'rt too far sold to hell:
It lies not in the compass of my prayers
To call thee back, yet let me counsel thee;
Persuade thy sister to some marriage.

Giovanni. Marriage? why that's to damn her; that's to prove
Her greedy of variety of lust.

Friar. O fearful! if thou wilt not, give me leave
To shrive her, lest she should die unabsolv'd.

Giovanni. At your best leisure, father: then she'll tell you,
How dearly she doth prize my matchless love;
Then you will know what pity 'twere we two
Should have been sunder'd from each other's arms.
View well her face, and in that little round
You may observe a world's variety;
For colour[29], lips: for sweet perfumes, her breath;
For jewels, eyes; for threads of purest gold,
Hair; for delicious choice of flowers, cheeks;
Wonder in every portion of that throne. —
Hear her but speak, and you will swear the spheres
Make music to the citizens in heaven. —
But, father, what is else for pleasure fram'd,
Lest I offend your ears, shall go unnam'd.

---

[29] For colour, lips. Dodsley reads for coral, lips; but the old copy is right; colour is placed in apposition to perfume. Just below he has form for throne. In the extravagance of Giovanni's praise, it is scarcely possible to know what terms he would adopt; but form appears too tame to be genuine, and frame occurs in the next verse but one. It is not quite clear to me, that a line has not been dropped after throne.

For world's variety, the old copy reads "world of variety," which spoils the metre. I suppose, the printer mistook the 's for o', the old abridgement of of. It would be unjust to say that the Friar has any thing in him of "the old squire of Troy;" yet he certainly betrays his duty both to God and man in the feeble resistance which he offers to the commencement and continuance of this fatal intercourse.

Friar. The more I hear, I pity thee the more;
   That one so excellent should give those parts
   All to a second death. What I can do,
   Is but to pray; and yet — I could advise thee,
   Wouldst thou be ruled.

Giovanni. In what?

Friar. Why leave her yet:
   The throne of mercy is above your trespass;
   Yet time is left you both —

Giovanni. To embrace each other,
   Else let all time be struck quite out of number;
   She is like me, and I like her, resolv'd.

Friar. No more! I'll visit her; — this grieves me most,
   Things being thus, a pair of souls are lost.

Exeunt.

SCENE VI.

A Room in Florio's House.

Enter Florio, Donado, Annabella, and Putana.

Florio. Where is Giovanni?

Annabella. Newly walk'd abroad,
      And, as I heard him say, gone to the friar,
      His reverend tutor.

Florio. That's a blessed man,
      A man made up of holiness; I hope
      He'll teach him how to gain another world.

Donado. Fair gentlewoman, here's a letter, sent To you from my young cousin[30]; I dare swear He loves you in his soul: would you could hear Sometimes, what I see daily, sighs and tears, As if his breast were prison to his heart.

Florio. Receive it, Annabella.

Annabella. Alas, good man!
Takes the Letter.

Donado. What's that she said?

Putana. An't please you, sir, she said, "Alas, good man!" Truly I do commend him to her every night before her first sleep, because I would have her dream of him; and she hearkens to that most religiously.

Donado. Say'st so? God a' mercy, Putana! there is something for thee — [*Gives her money*]— and prithee do what thou canst on his behalf; it shall not be lost labour, take my word for it.

Putana. Thank you most heartily, sir; now I have a feeling of your mind, let me alone to work.

---

[30] From my young cousin. Our author, like all the writers of his day, commonly uses cousin tor nephew and niece.

Annabella. Guardian.

Putana. Did you call?

Annabella. Keep this letter.

Donado. Signior Florio, in any case bid her read it instantly.

Florio. Keep it! for what? pray read it me here — right.

Annabella. I shall, sir. [She reads the Letter.

Donado. How do you find her inclined, signior?

Florio. Troth, sir, I know not how; not all so well As I could wish.

Annabella. Sir, I am bound to rest your cousin's debtor.
The jewel I'll return; for if he love,
I'll count that love a jewel.

Donado. Mark you that?
Nay, keep them both, sweet maid.

Annabella. You must excuse me,
Indeed I will not keep it.

Florio. Where's the ring,
That which your mother, in her will, bequeath'd,
And charged you on her blessing not to give it
To any but your husband? send back that[31].

Annabella. I have it not.

Florio. Ha! have it not; where is it?

Annabella. My brother in the morning took it from me,
Said he would wear it today.

---

[31] Send back that. Florio juggles strangely with his daughter's suitors. He tells Soranzo in Act I. that he had "his word engaged;" and yet he here endeavours to force her upon another! His subsequent conduct is not calculated to increase our respect for his character, or our sympathy for his overwhelming afflictions.

Florio. Well, what do you say
        To young Bergetto's love? are you content to
        Match with him? speak.

Donado. There is the point, indeed.

Annabella. What shall I do? I must say something now. [Aside.

Florio. What say? why do you not speak?

Annabella. Sir, with your leave — Please you to give me freedom?

Florio. Yes, you have [it.]

Annabella. Signior Donado, if your nephew mean
        To raise his better fortunes in his match,
        The hope of me will hinder such a hope:
        Sir, if you love him, as I know you do,
        Find one more worthy of his choice than me;
        In short, I'm sure I shall not be his wife.

Donado. Why here's plain dealing; I commend thee for't;
        And all the worst I wish thee, is, heaven bless thee!
        Your father yet and I will still be friends;
        Shall we not, Signior Florio?

Florio. Yes; why not?
        Look, here your cousin comes.

Enter Bergetto and Poggio.

Donado. Oh coxcomb! what doth he make here?

Bergetto. Where is my uncle, sirs?

Donado. What is the news now?

Bergetto. Save you, uncle, save you! You must not think I come for nothing,
        masters; and how, and how is it? what, you have read my letter? ah,
        there I— tickled you, i'faith.

Poggio. But 'twere better you had tickled her in another place.

Bergetto. Sirrah sweetheart, I'll tell thee a good jest; and riddle what it is.

Annabella. You say you'll tell me.

Bergetto. As I was walking just now in the street, I met a swaggering fellow would needs take the wall of me; and because he did thrust me, I very valiantly call'd him rogue; he hereupon bade me draw, I told him I had more wit than so: but when he saw that I would not, he did so maul me with the hilts of his rapier, that my head sung whilst my feet caper'd in the kennel.

Donado. Was ever the like ass seen!

Annabella. And what did you all this while?

Bergetto. Laugh at him for a gull, till I saw the blood run about mine ears, and then I could not choose but find in my heart to cry; till a fellow with a broad beard (they say he is a new-come doctor) call'd me into his house, and gave me a plaster, look you, here 'tis; — and, sir, there was a young wench wash'd my face and hands most excellently; i'faith I shall love her as long as I live for it — did she not, Poggio?

Poggio. Yes, and kiss'd him too.

Bergetto. Why la now, you think I tell a lie, uncle, I warrant.

Donado. Would he that beat thy blood out of thy head, had beaten some wit into it! for I fear thou never wilt have any.

Bergetto. Oh uncle, but there was a wench would have done a man's heart good to have look'd on her. By this light, she had a face methinks worth twenty of you, Mistress Annabella.

Donado. Was ever such a fool born?

Annabella. I am glad she liked you[32], sir.

Bergetto. Are you so? by my troth I thank you, forsooth.

---

[32] I am glad she lik'd you, i.e. pleased you. So in Lear, "His face likes me not." Maid's Tragedy, Act ii. "What look likes you best."— Reed.

Florio. Sure it was the doctor's niece, that was last day with us here.

Bergetto. 'Twas she, 'twas she.

Donado. How do you know that, Simplicity?

Bergetto. Why does he not say so? if I should have said no, I should have given him the lie, uncle, and so have deserv'd a dry beating again; I'll none of that.

Florio. A very modest well-behav'd young maid, as I have seen.

Donado. Is she indeed?

Florio. Indeed she is, if I have any judgment.

Donado. Well, sir, now you are free: you need not care for sending letters now; you are dismiss'd, your mistress here will none of you.

Bergetto. No! why what care I for that? I can have wenches enough in Parma for half a crown a-piece; cannot I, Poggio?

Poggio. I'll warrant you, sir.

Donado. Signior Florio, I thank you for your free recourse you gave for my admittance; and to you, fair maid, that jewel I will give you against your marriage. Come, will you go, sir?

Bergetto. Ay, marry will I. Mistress, farewell, mistress; I'll come again tomorrow — farewell, mistress.

Exeunt Donado, Bergetto, and Poggio.

Enter Giovanni.

Florio. Son, where have you been? what, alone, alone still?
I would not have it so; you must forsake
This over-bookish humour. Well; your sister
Hath shook the fool off.

Giovanni. 'Twas no match for her.

Florio. 'Twas not indeed; I meant it nothing less;

Soranzo is the man I only like;
Look on him, Annabella. Come, 'tis supper-time,
And it grows late. [Exit.

Giovanni. Whose jewel's that?

Annabella. Some sweetheart's.

Giovanni. So I think.

Annabella. A lusty youth,
Signior Donado, gave it me to wear
Against my marriage.

Giovanni. But you shall not wear it;
Send it him back again.

Annabella. What, you are jealous?

Giovanni. That you shall know anon, at better leisure:
Welcome sweet night! the evening crowns the day.

Exeunt.

ACT III.
SCENE I.

A Room in Donado's House.

Enter Bergetto and Poggio.

Bergetto. Does my uncle think to make me a baby still? No, Poggio; he shall know I have a sconce now.

Poggio. Ay, let him not bob you off like an ape with an apple.

Bergetto. 'Sfoot, I will have the wench, if he were ten uncles, in despite of his nose, Poggio.

Poggio. Hold him to the grindstone, and give not a jot of ground; she hath in a manner promised you already.

Bergetto. True, Poggio; and her uncle, the doctor, swore I should marry her.

Poggio. He swore; I remember.

Bergetto. And I will have her, that's more: did'st see the codpiece-point she gave me, and the box of marmalade?

Poggio. Very well; andkiss'd you, that my chops water'd at the sight on't: there is no way but to clap up a marriage in hugger-mugger.

Bergetto. I will do it; for I tell thee, Poggio, I begin to grow valiant methinks, and my courage begins to rise.

Poggio. Should you be afraid of your uncle?

Bergetto. Hang him, old doating rascal! no; I say I will have her.

Poggio. Lose no time then.

Bergetto. I will beget a race of wise men and constables that shall cart whores at their own charges; and break the duke's peace ere I have done, myself. — Come away.

Exeunt.

SCENE II.

A Room in Florio's House.

Enter Florio, Giovanni, Soraxzo, Anxabella, Putana, and Vasques.

Florio. My lord Soranzo, though I must confess
    The proffers that are made me have been great,
    In marriage of my daughter; yet the hope
    Of your Still rising honours has prevail'd
    Above all other jointures: here she is;
    She knows my mind; speak for yourself to her,
    And hear you, daughter, see you use him nobly:
    For any private speech, I'll give you time.
    Come, son, and you the rest; let them alone;
    Agree [they] as they may.

Soranzo. I thank you, sir.

Giovanni. Sister, be not all woman, think on me. [Aside to Ann.

Soranzo. Vasques.

Vasques. My lord.

Soranzo. Attend me without

Exeunt all but Soranzo and Annabella.

Annabella. Sir, what's your will with me?

Soranzo. Do you not know What I should tell you?

Annabella. Yes; you'll say you love me.

Soranzo. And I will swear it too; will you believe it?

Annabella. Tis no point of faith.

Enter Giovanni, in the Gallery, above.

Soranzo. Have you not will to love?

Annabella. Not you.

53

Soranzo. Whom then?

Annabella. That's as the fates infer.

Giovanni. Of those I'm regent now.

Soranzo. What mean you, sweet?

Annabella. To live and die a maid.

Soranzo. Oh, that's unfit.

Giovanni. Here's one can say that's but a woman's note.

Soranzo. Did you but see my heart, then would you swear

Annabella. That you were dead.

Giovanni. That's true, or somewhat near it.

Soranzo. See you these true love's tears?

Annabella. No.

Giovanni. Now she winks.

Soranzo. They plead to you for grace.

Annabella. Yet nothing speak.

Soranzo. Oh, grant my suit.

Annabella. What is't?

Soranzo. To let me live —

Annabella. Take it.

Soranzo. Still yours.

Annabella. That is not mine to give.

Giovanni. One such another word would kill his hopes.

Soranzo. Mistress, to leave those fruitless strifes of wit,
      Know I have lov'd you long, and lov'd you truly:
      Not hope of what you have, but what you are,
      Hath drawn me on; then let me not in vain
      Still feel the rigour of your chaste disdain:
      I'm sick, and sick to the heart.

Annabella. Help, aqua vitae!

Soranzo. What mean you?

Annabella. Why, I thought you had been sick.

Soranzo. Do you mock my love?

Giovanni. There, sir, she was too nimble.

Soranzo. Tis plain; she laughs at me. — [*Aside.*]
      These scornful taunts
      Neither become your modesty or years.

Annabella. You are no looking-glass; or if you were,
      I would dress my language by you.

Giovanni. I am confirm'd.

Annabella. To put you out of doubt, my lord, methinks
      Your common sense should make you understand,
      That if I lov'd you, or desired your love,
      Some way I should have given you better taste:
      But since you are a nobleman, and one
      I would not wish should spend his youth in hopes,
      Let me advise you to forbear your suit,
      And think I wish you well, I tell you this.

Soranzo. Is't you speak this?

Annabella. Yes, I myself; yet know,
      (Thus far I give you comfort) if mine eyes
      Could have pick'd out a man, amongst all those
      That sued to me, to make a husband of,

You should have been that man; let this suffice,
Be noble in your secrecy, and wise.

Giovanni. Why, now I see she loves me.

Annabella. One word more.
As ever virtue liv'd within your mind,
As ever noble courses were your guide,
As ever you would have me know you lov'd me,
Let not my father know hereof by you:
If I hereafter find that I must marry,
It shall be you or none.

Soranzo. I take that promise.

Annabella. Oh, oh my head!

Soranzo. What's the matter, not well?

Annabella. Oh, I begin to sicken.

Giovanni. Heaven forbid! [Exit from above.

Soranzo. Help, help, within there, ho!

Enter Florio, Giovanni, and Putana.

Look to your daughter[33], Signior Florio.

Florio. Hold her up, she swoons.

Giovanni. Sister, how do you?

Annabella. Sick — brother, are you there?

Florio. Convey her to bed instantly, whilst I send for a physician; quickly, I say.

Putana. Alas, poor child!

---

[33] Look to your daughter. The old copy gives this speech to the brother. It is evidently a continuation of Soronzo's call for assistance.

Exeunt all but Soranzo.

Re-enter Vasques.

Vasques. My lord.

Soranzo. Oh, Vasques! now I doubly am undone,
        Both in my present and my future hopes:
        She plainly told me that she could not love,
        And thereupon soon sicken'd; and I fear
        Her life's in danger.

Vasques. By'r lady, sir, and so is yours, if you knew all. [*Aside.*] —'Las, sir, I
        am sorry for that; may be, 'tis but the maids-sickness, an over-flux of
        youth; and then, sir, there is no such present remedy as present
        marriage. But hath she given you an absolute denial?

Soranzo. She hath, and she hath not; I'm full of grief;
        But what she said, I'll tell thee as we go.

Exeunt.

SCENE III.

Another Room in the same.

Enter Giovanni and Putana.

Putana. Oh, sir, we are all undone, quite undone, utterly undone, and shamed for ever: your sister, oh your sister!

Giovanni. What of her? for heaven's sake, speak; how does she?

Putana. Oh that ever I was born to see this day!

Giovanni. She is not dead, ha? is she?

Putana. Dead! no, she is quick; —'tis worse, she is with child. You know what you have done; heaven forgive you! 'tis too late to repent now, heaven help us!

Giovanni. With child? how dost thou know't?

Putana. How do I know't? am I at these years ignorant what the meanings of qualms and water — pangs be? of changing of colours, queasiness of stomachs, pukings, and another thing that I could name? Do not, for her and your credit's sake, spend the time in asking how, and which way, 'tis so: she is quick, upon my word; if you let a physician see her water, you are undone.

Giovanni. But in what case is she?

Putana. Prettily amended: 'twas but a fit, which I soon espied, and she must look for often henceforward.

Giovanni. Commend me to her, bid her take no care[34];
Let not the doctor visit her, I charge you;
Make some excuse, till I return. — Oh me!
I have a world of business in my head.
Do not discomfort her —
How do these news perplex me! If my father
Come to her, tell him she's recover'd well;
Say 'twas but some ill diet — d'ye hear, woman?

---

[34] Bid her take no care. i. e. bid her not lo be too anxious, or apprehensive.

Look you to't.

Putana. I will, sir.

Exeunt.

SCENE IV.

Another Room in the same.

Enter Florio and Richardetto.

Florio. And how do you find her, sir?

Richardetto. Indifferent well;
      I see no danger, scarce perceive she's sick,
      But that she told me, she had lately eaten
      Melons, and, as she thought, those disagree'd
      With her young stomach.

Florio. Did you give her aught?

Richardetto. An easy surfeit-water, nothing else;
      You need not doubt her health; I rather think
      Her sickness is a fulness of her blood —
      You understand me?

Florio. I do; you counsel well;
      And once, within these few days, will so order it,
      She shall be married ere she know the time.

Richardetto. Yet let not haste, sir, make unworthy choice:
      That were dishonour.

Florio. Master doctor, no;
      I will not do so neither: in plain words,
      My Lord Soranzo is the man I mean.

Richardetto. A noble and a virtuous gentleman.

Florio. As any is in Parma: not far hence,
      Dwells Father Bonaventure, a grave friar,
      Once tutor to my son; now at his cell
      I'll have them married.

Richardetto. You have plotted wisely.

Florio. I'll send one straight to speak with him to-night.

Richardetto. Soranzo's wise; he will delay no time.

Florio. It shall be so.

Enter Friar and Giovanni.

Friar. Good peace be here, and love!

Florio. Welcome, religious friar; you are one
      That still bring blessing to the place you come to.

Giovanni. Sir, with what speed I could, I did my best
      To draw this holy man from forth his cell,
      To visit my sick sister'; that with words
      Of ghostly comfort, in this time of need,
      He might absolve her, whether she live or die.

Florio. Twas well done, Giovanni; thou herein
      Hast show'd a Christian's care, a brother's love:
      Come, father, I'll conduct you to her chamber,
      And one thing would entreat you.

Friar. Say on, sir.

Florio. I have a father's dear impression,
      And wish, before I fall into my grave,
      That I might see her married, as 'tis fit;
      A word from you, grave man, will win her more
      Than all our best persuasions.

Friar. Gentle sir,
      All this I'll say, that Heaven may prosper her.

Exeunt.

SCENE V.

A Room in Richaudetto's House.

Enter Grimaldi.

Grimaldi. Now if the doctor keep his word, Soranzo,
      Twenty to one you miss your bride. I know
      Tis an unhoble act, and not becomes
      A soldier's valour; but in terms of love,
      Where merit cannot sway, policy must:
      I am resolv'd, if this physician
      Play not on both hands, then Soranzo falls.

Enter Richardetto.

Richardetto. You are come as I could wish; this very night
      Soranzo, 'tis ordain'd, must be affied
      To Annabella, and, for aught I know,
      Married.

Grimaldi. How!

Richardetto. Yet your patience;
      The place, 'tis friar Bonaventure's cell.
      Now I would wish you to bestow this night
      In watching thereabouts; 'tis but a night:—
      If you miss now, tomorrow I'll know all.

Grimaldi. Have you the poison?

Richardetto. Here 'tis, in this box;
      Doubt nothing, this will do't; in any case,
      As you respect your life, be quick and sure.

Grimaldi. I'll speed him.

Richardetto. Do. — Away; for 'tis not safe
      You should be seen much here — ever my love!

Grimaldi. And mine to you. *Exit.*

Richardetto. So! if this hit, I'll laugh and hug revenge;
      And they that now dream of a wedding-feast,

May chance to mourn the lusty bridegroom's ruin:
But to my other business — niece Philotis!

Enter Philotis.

Philotis. Uncle.

Richardetto. My lovely niece, You have bethought you?

Philotis. Yes — and, as you counsell'd,
    Fashion'd my heart to love him; but he swears
    He will to-night be married; for he fears
    His uncle else, if he should know the drift,
    Will hinder all, and call his coz to shrift.

Richardetto. To-night? why best of all; but let me see,
    I— ha! — yes — so it shall be; in disguise
    We'll early to the friar's — I have thought on't.

Philotis. Uncle, he comes.

Enter Bergetto and Poggio.

Richardetto. Welcome, my worthy coz.

Bergetto. Lass, pretty lass, come buss, lass! A-ha, Poggio!
Kisses her.

Richardetto. There's hope of this yet[35]. [*Aside.*]
    You shall have time enough; withdraw a little,
    We must confer at large.

Bergetto. Have you not sweetmeats, or dainty devices for me?

Philotis. You shall [have] enough, sweetheart.

Bergetto. Sweetheart! mark that, Poggio. By my troth I cannot choose but
    kiss thee once more for that word, sweetheart. Poggio, I have a
    monstrous swelling about my stomach, whatsoever the matter be.

---

[35] There's hope of this yet.] The 4to erroneously gives this hemistich to Philotis. If it be not a side-speech of the uncle, it must be considered as a continuation of poor Poggio's rapture at the condescension of his mistress.

Poggio. You shall have physic for't, sir.

Richardetto. Time runs apace.

Bergetto. Time's a blockhead.

Richardetto. Be ruled; when we have done what's fit to do,
  Then you may kiss your fill, and bed her too.

Exeunt.

SCENE VI.

Florio's House.

Annabella's Chamber. A Table with Wax Lights; Annabella at Confession before the Friar; she weeps and wrings her hands.

Friar. I am glad to see this penance; for, believe me,
      You have unripp'd a soul so foul and guilty,
      As I must tell you true, I marvel how
      The earth hath borne you up; but weep, weep on,
      These tears may do you good; weep faster yet,
      Whilst I do read a lecture.

Annabella. Wretched creature!

Friar. Ay, you are wretched, miserably wretched,
      Almost condemn'd alive. There is a place,
      List, daughter! in a black and hollow vault,
      Where day is never seen; there shines no sun,
      But flaming horror of consuming fires,
      A lightless sulphur, choak'd with smoky fogs
      Of an infected darkness: in this place
      Dwell many thousand thousand sundry sorts
      Of never-dying deaths: there damned souls
      Roar without pity; there are gluttons fed
      With toads and adders; there is burning oil
      Pour'd down the drunkard's throat; the usurer
      Is forced to sup whole draughts of molten gold;
      There is the murderer for ever stabb'd,
      Yet can he never die; there lies the wanton
      On racks of burning steel, whilst in his soul
      He feels the torment of his raging lust. —

Annabella. Mercy! oh mercy!

Friar. There stand these wretched things,
      Who have dream'd out whole years in lawless sheets
      And secret incests, cursing one another:
      Then you will wish each kiss your brother gave,
      Had been a dagger's point; then you shall hear
      How he will cry, "Oh, would my wicked sister
      Had first been damn'd, when she did yield to lust!"—
      But soft, methinks I see repentance work

New motions in your heart; say, how is't with you?

Annabella. Is there no way left to redeem my miseries?

Friar. There is, despair not; Heaven is merciful,
   And offers grace even now. Tis thus agreed:
   First, for your honour's safety, that you marry
   My lord Soranzo; next, to save your soul,
   Leave off this life, and henceforth live to him.

Annabella. Ah me!

Friar. Sigh not; I know the baits of sin
   Are hard to leave; oh, 'tis a death to do't.
   Remember what must come: are you content?

Annabella. I am.

Friar. I like it well; we'll take the time.
   Who's near us there?

Enter Florio and Giovanni.

Florio. Did you call, father?

Friar. Is lord Soranzo come?

Florio. He stays below.

Friar. Have you acquainted him at full?

Florio. I have,
   And he is overjoy'd.

Friar. And so are we:
   Bid him come near.

Giovanni. My sister weeping? — Ha!
   I fear this friar's falsehood. [*Aside.*] — I will call him. [Exit.

Florio. Daughter, are you resolv'd?

Annabella. Father, I am.

Re-enter Giovanni with Soranzo and Vasques.

Florio. My lord Soranzo, here
      Give me your hand; for that, I give you this.
Joins their hands.

Soranzo. Lady, say you so too?

Annabella. I do, and vow
      To live with you and your's.

Friar. Timely resolv'd;
      My blessing rest on both! more to be done,
      You may perform it on the morning-sun.

Exeunt.

SCENE VII.

The Street before the Monastery.

Enter Grimaldi with his Rapier drawn, and a dark Lantern.

Grimaldi. Tis early night as yet, and yet too soon
    To finish such a work; here I will lie
    To listen who comes next. [He lies down.

Enter Bergetto and Philotis disguised; and followed, at a distance, by Richardetto and Poggio.

Bergetto. We are almost at the place, I hope, sweetheart.

Grimaldi. I hear them near, and heard one say "sweetheart."
    Tis he; now guide my hand, some angry justice,
    Home to his bosom. — Now have at you, sir!

Stabs Bergetto, and exit.

Bergetto. Oh help, help! here's a stitch fallen in my guts; oh for a flesh-tailor
    quickly — Poggio!

Philotis. What ails my love?

Bergetto. I am sure I cannot piss forward and backward, and yet I am wet
    before and behind; lights! lights! ho, lights!

Philotis. Alas, some villain here has slain my love.

Richardetto. Oh Heaven forbid it; raise up the next neighbours
    Instantly, Poggio, and bring lights. — [*Exit Pog.*]
    How is't, Bergetto? slain! It cannot be;
    Are you sure you are hurt?

Bergetto. O my belly seethes like a porridge-pot; some cold water, I shall boil
    over else: my whole body is in a sweat, that you may wring my shirt;
    feel here — why, Poggio!

Re-enter Poggio, with Officers, and Lights.

Poggio. Here; alas! how do you?

Richardetto. Give me a light. What's here? all blood! O sirs,
      Signior Donado's nephew now is slain.
      Follow the murderer with all the haste
      Up to the city, he cannot be far hence;
      Follow, I beseech you.

      Officers. Follow, follow, follow.
Exeunt.

Richardetto. Tear off thy linen, coz, to stop his wounds; Be of good
      comfort, man.

Bergetto. Is all this mine own blood? nay, then, good night with me. Poggio,
      commend me to my uncle, dost hear? bid him, for my sake, make
      much of this wench: oh — I am going the wrong way sure, my belly
      aches so — oh farewell, Poggio! — oh! — oh! — [Dies.

Philotis. O he is dead.

Poggio. How! dead!

Richardetto. He's dead indeed;
      Tis now too late to weep: let's have him home,
      And, with what speed we may, find out the murderer.

Poggio. Oh my master! my master! my master!

Exeunt.

SCENE VIII.

A Room in Hippolita's House.

Enter Vasques and Hippolita.

Hippolita. Betroth'd?

Vasques. I saw it.

Hippolita. And when's the marriage-day?

Vasques. Some two days hence.

Hippolita. Two days! why man I would but wish two hours,
    To send him to his last, and lasting sleep;
    And, Vasques, thou shalt see I'll do it bravely.

Vasques. I do not doubt your wisdom, nor, I trust, you my secrecy; I am
    infinitely yours.

Hippolita. I will be thine in spite of my disgrace.
    So soon? O wicked man! I durst be sworn,
    He'd laugh to see me weep.

Vasques. And that's a villainous fault in him.

Hippolita. No, let him laugh; I am arm'd in my resolves:
    Be thou still true.

Vasques. I should get little by treachery against so hopeful a preferment, as I
    am like to climb to —

Hippolita. Even to — my bosom, Vasques. Let my youth
    Revel in these new pleasures; if we thrive,
    He now hath but a pair of days to live.

Exeunt.

SCENE IX.

The Street before the Cardinal's Gates.

Enter Florio, Donado, Richardetto, Poggio, and Officers.

Florio. Tis bootless now to shew yourself a child,
    Signior Donado, what is done, is done
    Spend not the time in tears, but seek for justice.

Richardetto. I must confess, somewhat I was in fault,
    That had not first acquainted you what love
    Past 'twixt him and my niece; but, as I live,
    His fortune grieves me as it were mine own.

Donado. Alas, poor creature, he meant no man harm,
    That I am sure of.

Florio. I believe that too.
    But stay, my masters; are you sure you saw
    The murderer pass here?

Officer. An it please you, sir, we are sure we saw a ruffian, with a naked
    weapon in his hand all bloody, get into my lord Cardinal's Grace's
    gate; that we are sure of; but for fear of his grace (bless us!) we durst
    go no farther.

Donado. Know you what manner of man he was?

Officer. Yes sure, I know the man; they say he is a soldier: he that lov'd your
    daughter, sir, an't please ye; 'twas he for certain.

Florio. Grimaldi, on my life.

Officer. Ay, ay, the same.

Richardetto. The Cardinal is noble; he no doubt
    Will give true justice.

Donado. Knock some one at the gate.

Poggio. I'll knock, sir. [Knocks.

Servant. [*within*] What would ye?

71

Florio. We require speech with the lord Cardinal
　　　　About some present business; pray inform
　　　　His grace, that we are here.

Enter Cardinal, followed by Grimaldi.

Cardinal. Why how now, friends! what saucy mates are you,
　　　　That know nor duty nor civility?
　　　　Are we a person fit to be your host;
　　　　Or is our house become your common inn,
　　　　To — beat our doors at pleasure? What such haste
　　　　Is yours, as that it cannot wait fit times?
　　　　Are you the masters of this commonwealth,
　　　　And know no more discretion? Oh, your news
　　　　Is here before you; you have lost a nephew,
　　　　Donado, last night by Grimaldi slain:
　　　　Is that your business? well, sir, we have knowledge on't,
　　　　Let that suffice.

Grimaldi. In presence of your grace,
　　　　In thought, I never meant Bergetto harm:
　　　　But, Florio, you can tell, with how much scorn
　　　　Soranzo, back'd with his confederates,
　　　　Hath often wrong'd me; I to be reveng'd,
　　　　(For that I could but win him else to fight)
　　　　Had thought, by way of ambush, to have kill'd him,
　　　　But was, unluckily, therein mistook;
　　　　Else he had felt what late Bergetto did:
　　　　And though my fault to him were merely chance,
　　　　Yet humbly I submit me to your grace, [Kneeling.
　　　　To do with me as you please.

Cardinal. Rise up, Grimaldi. [He rises.
　　　　You citizens of Parma, if you seek
　　　　For justice, know, as Nuncio from the pope,
　　　　For this offence I here receive Grimaldi
　　　　Into his Holiness' protection:
　　　　He is no common man, but nobly born,
　　　　Of princes' blood, though you, sir Florio,
　　　　Thought him too mean a husband for your daughter.
　　　　If more you seek. for, you must go to Rome,
　　　　For he shall thither; learn more wit for shame, —

Bury your dead:— away, Grimaldi — leave 'em!

Exeunt Cardinal and Grimaldi.

Donado. Is this a churchman's voice? dwells justice here?

Florio. Justice is fled to heaven, and comes no nearer.
        Soranzo? — was't for him? O impudence!
        Had he the face to speak it, and not blush?
        Come, come, Donado, there's no help in this,
        When cardinals think murder's not amiss:
        Great men may do their wills, we must obey,
        But Heaven will judge them for't, another day.

Exeunt.

ACT IV.
SCENE I.[36]

A Room in Florio's House. — A Banquet set out. — Hautboys.

Enter the Friar, Giovanni, Annabella, Philotis, Soranzo, Donado, Florio, Richardetto, Putana, and Vasques.

Friar. These holy rites perform'd, now take your times
     To spend the remnant of the day in feast;
     Such fit repasts are pleasing to the saints,
     Who are your guests, though not with mortal eyes
     To be beheld. — Long prosper in this day,
     You happy couple, to each other's joy!

Soranzo. Father, your prayer is heard; the hand of goodness
     Hath been a shield for me against my death;
     And, more to bless me, hath enrich'd my life
     With this most precious jewel; such a prize
     As earth hath not another like to this.
     Cheer up, my love; and, gentlemen, my friends.
     Rejoice with me in mirth: this day we'll crown
     With lusty cups to Annabella's health.

Giovanni. Oh torture! were the marriage yet undone,
     Ere I'd endure this sight, to see my love
     Glipt by another, I would dare confusion,
     And stand the horror of ten thousand deaths.
Aside.

Vasques. Are you not well, sir?

Giovanni. Prithee, fellow, wait;
     I need not thy officious diligence.

Florio. Signior Donado, come, you must forget

---

[36] I have reluctantly followed the 4to, (which has no division of scenes,) and begun the fourth Act here. The reader will see, as he proceeds, the impropriety of this arrangement. After all, there is but a choice of evils; for as some time must necessarily have elapsed (two days according to Vasques) since the death of Poggio, sufficient would hardly be gained on the score of probability to justify disturbing the author's distribution of the story; though it might be wished-that this scene had concluded the third Act.

Your late mishaps, and drown your cares in wine.

Soranzo. Vasques!

Vasques. My lord.

Soranzo. Reach me that weighty bowl.
     Here, brother Giovanni, here's to you,
     Your turn comes next, though now a bachelor;
     Here's to your sister's happiness, and mine!
Drinks, and offers him the bowl.

Giovanni. I cannot drink.

Soranzo. What!

Giovanni. 'Twill indeed offend me.

Annabella. Pray do not urge him, if he be not willing.
Hautboys.

Florio. How now! what noise is this?

Vasques. O sir, I had forgot to tell you; certain young maidens of Parma, in
     honour to madam Annabella's marriage, have sent their loves to her
     in a Masque, for which they humbly crave your patience and silence.

Soranzo. We are much bound to them; so much the more,
     As it comes unexpected: guide them in.

Enter Hippolita, followed by Ladies in white Robes with Garlands of Willows, all masked.

Music And A Dance.

Soranzo. Thanks, lovely virgins! now might we but know
     To whom we have been beholding for [this] love,
     We shall acknowledge it.

Hippolita. Yes, you shall know:
     What think you now?
Unmasks.

Omnes. Hippolita!

Hippolita. Tis she;
        Be not amaz'd; nor blush, young lovely bride,
        I come not to defraud you of your man:
        Tis now no time to reckon up the talk
        What Parma long hath rumour'd of us both;
        Let rash report run on! the breath that vents it
        Will, like a bubble, break itself at last.
        But now to you, sweet creature; — lend your hand —
        Perhaps it hath been said, that I would claim
        Some interest in Soranzo, now your lord;
        What I have right to do, his soul knows best:
        But in my duty to your noble worth,
        Sweet Annabella, and my care of you,
        .Here, take, Soranzo, take this hand from me,
        I'll once more join, what by the holy church
        Is finished and allow'd. — Have I done well?

Soranzo. You have too much engaged us.

Hippolita. One thing more.
        That you may know my single charity[37]
        Freely I here remit all interest
        I e'er could claim, and give you back your vows;
        And to confirm't — reach me a cup of wine —
        [Vasques gives her a poisoned cup.
        My lord Soranzo, in this draught I drink
        Long rest t' ye! —[*she drinks*]— look to it, Vasques.
Aside.

Vasques. Fear nothing —

Soranzo. Hippolita, I thank you; and will pledge
        This happy union as another life.
        Wine, there!

Vasques. You shall have none; neither shall you pledge her.

Hippolita. How!

---

[37] My single charity. i. e. pure, genuine, disinterested charity.

Vasques. Know now, mistress she-devil, your own mischievous treachery
       hath kill'd you; I must not marry you.

Hippolita. Villain!

Omnes. What's the matter?

Vasques. Foolish woman, thou art now like a firebrand, that hath kindled
       others and burnt thyself:— troppo sperar, inganna — thy vain hope
       hath deceived thee; thou art but dead; if thou hast any grace, pray.

Hippolita. Monster!

Vasques. Die in charity, for shame. — This thing of malice, this woman,
       hath privately corrupted me with promise of [marriage,] under this
       politic reconciliation, to poison my lord, whilst she might laugh at his
       confusion on his marriage-day. I promised her fair; but I knew what
       my reward should have been, and would willingly have spared her
       life, but that I was acquainted with the danger of her disposition; and
       now have fitted her a just payment in her own coin: there she is, she
       hath yet[38] — and end thy days in peace, vile woman; as for life,
       there's no hope, think not on't.

Omnes. Wonderful justice!

Richardetto. Heaven, thou art righteous.

Hippolita. O 'tis true,
       I feel my minute coming. Had that slave
       Kept promise — O my torment! — thou, this hour,
       Hadst dy'd, Soranzo — heat above hell-fire! —
       Yet, ere I pass away — cruel, cruel flames! —
       Take here my curse amongst you; may thy bed
       Of marriage be a rack unto thy heart,
       Burn blood, and boil in vengeance — O my heart,
       My flame's intolerable — may'st thou live
       To father bastards; may her womb bring forth
       Monsters — and die together in your sins,

---

[38] She hath yet. The old copy has a considerable double break here, probably from some
defect in the M.S.

Hated, scorn'd, and unpitied! — oh — oh —
Dies.

Florio. Was e'er so vile a creature!

Richardetto. Here's the end
Of lust and pride.

Annabella. It is a fearful sight.

Soranzo. Vasques, I know thee now a trusty servant,
And never will forget thee. — Come, my love,
We'll home, and thank the heavens for this escape.
Father and friends, we must break up this mirth;
It is too sad a feast.

Donado. Bear hence the body.

Friar. [*Aside to Gio.*] Here's an ominous change!
Mark this, my Giovanni, and take heed! —
I fear the event; that marriage seldom's good,
Where the bride-banquet so begins in blood.

Exeunt.

SCENE II[39].

A Room in Richardetto's House.

Enter Richardetto and Philotis.

Richardetto. My wretched wife, more wretched in her shame
       Than in her wrongs to me, hath paid too soon
       The forfeit of her modesty and life.
       And I am sure, my niece, though vengeance hover,
       Keeping aloof yet from Soranzo's fall,
       Yet he will fall, and sink with his own weight.
       I need not now (my heart persuades me so,)
       To further his confusion; there is One
       Above begins to work; for, as I hear,
       Debates already 'twixt his wife and him
       Thicken and run to head; she, as 'tis said,
       Slightens his love, and he abandons her's:
       Much talk I hear. Since things go thus, my niece,
       In tender love and pity of your youth,
       My counsel is, that you should free your years
       From hazard of these woes, by flying hence
       To fair Cremona, there to vow your soul
       In holiness, a holy votaress;
       Leave me to see the end of these extremes.
       All human worldly courses are uneven,
       No life is blessed but the way to heaven.

Philotis. Uncle, shall I resolve to be a nun?

Richardetto. Ay, gentle niece; and in your hourly prayers
       Remember me, your poor unhappy uncle.
       Hie to Cremona now, as fortune leads,

---

[39] Scene II. As the play is now divided, this conversation takes place on the way home from the marriage-feast, or immediately after it; and, in either case, before Richardetto could have heard a word of what he informs his niece —

Debates already 'twixt his wife and him thicken and run to head; she, as 'tis said, slightens his love, and he abandons hers: Much talk I hear.

Enough, and more than enough of improbability would perhaps remain, were even the arrangement recommended in a former page to take place; but the most glaring part ot it would certainly be removed or weakened by the change.

Your home your cloister, your best friends your beads;
Your chaste and single life shall crown your birth,
Who dies a virgin, lives a saint on earth.

Philotis. Then farewell, world, and worldly thoughts, adieu!
Welcome, chaste vows, myself I yield to you.

Exeunt.

SCENE III.

A Chamber in Soranzo's House.

Enter Soranzo unbraced, and dragging in Annabella.

Soranzo. Come, strumpet, famous whore! were every drop
      Of blood that runs in thy adulterous veins
      A life, this sword (dost see't?) should in one blow
      Confound them all. Harlot, rare, notable harlot,
      That with thy brazen face maintain'st thy sin,
      Was there no man in Parma to be bawd
      To your loose cunning whoredom else but I?
      Must your hot itch and pleurisy of lust,
      The heyday of your luxury,[40] be fed
      Up to a surfeit, and could none but I
      Be pick'd out to be cloak to your close tricks,
      Your belly-sports? — Now I must be the dad
      To all that gallimaufry that is stuff'd
      In thy corrupted bastard-bearing womb! —
      Why, must I?[41]

Annabella. Beastly man! Why? —'tis thy fate.
      I sued not to thee; for, but that I thought
      Your over-loving lordship would have run
      Mad on denial, had you lent me time,
      I would have told you in what case I was:
      But you would needs be doing.

Soranzo. Whore of whores!
      Darest thou tell me this?

Annabella. O yes; why not?
      You were deceived in me; 'twas not for love
      I chose you, but for honour; yet know this,
      Would you be patient yet, and hide your shame,
      I'd see whether I could love you.

---

[40] The heyday of your luxury, i. e. the height of your wantonness. — Reed. Luxury, about which the commentators on Shakspeare have drivelled out so much indecency, is simply, the French luxure, the old word for lust, and common to every writer of the poet's age. Luxury, in the present sense of the word, is their luxe.

[41] Why, must I? The 4to is corrupt in this place, and reads, Shey, must I? Dodsley has corrected it into Say; but I prefer the expression in the text, as it seems borne out by Annabclla's answer.

Soranzo. Excellent quean!
    Why, art thou not with child?

Annabella. What needs all this,
    When 'tis superfluous? I confess I am.

Soranzo. Tell me by whom.

Annabella. Soft,[42] 'twas not in my bargain.
    Yet somewhat, sir, to stay your longing stomach
    I am content t' acquaint you with; The man,
    The more than man, that got this sprightly boy —
    (For 'tis a boy, [and] therefore glory, sir,[43]
    Your heir shall be a son)—

Soranzo. Damnable monster!

Annabella. Nay, an you will not hear, I'll speak no more.

Soranzo. Yes speak, and speak thy last.

Annabella. A match, a match!
    This noble creature was in every part
    So angel-like, so glorious, that a woman,
    Who had not been but human, as was I,
    Would have kneel'd to him, and have begg'd for love. —
    You! why you are not worthy once to name
    His name without true worship, or, indeed,
    Unless you kneel'd, to hear another name him.

Soranzo. What was he call'd?

Annabella. We are not come to that;
    Let it suffice, that you shall have the glory
    To father what so brave a father got.

---

[42] Soft, sir. I have omitted sir, which spoils the verse, and appears to have crept in from the line immediately below it.

[43] therefore glory, sir, This is made out by Dodsley from the old copy, which reads, "For 'tis a boy that for glory, sir;" and has all the appearance of being genuine. The insulting and profligate language of this wretched woman, if not assumed, like that of Bianca in Lore's Sacrifice, to provoke her husband to destroy her on the spot, is perfectly loathsome and detestable. Well sung the poet — nihil est audacius illis deprensis: iram atque animos a crimine summit.

In brief, had not this chance fall'n out 'as it doth,
I never had been troubled with a thought
That you had been a creature; — but for marriage,
I scarce dream yet of that.

Soranzo. Tell me his name.

Annabella. Alas, alas, there's all! will you believe?

Soranzo. What?

Annabella. You shall never know.

Soranzo. How!

Annabella. Never; if
    You do, let me curs'd.

Soranzo. Not know it, strumpet! I'll rip up thy heart,
    And find it there.

Annabella. Do, do.

Soranzo. And with my teeth,
    Tear the prodigious letcher joint by joint.

Annabella. Ha, ha, ha! the man's merry.

Soranzo. Dost thou laugh?
    Come, whore, tell me your lover, or by truth
    I'll hew thy flesh to shreds; who is't?

Annabella. Che morte pin dolce che morirepcr amore? [*Sings.*

Soranzo. Thus will I pull thy hair, and thus I'll drag
    Thy lust be-leper'd body through the dust — [*Hales her up and down.*]
    Yet tell his name.

Annabella. Morendo in grazia dee morire senza dolore[44]. [*Sings.*]

---

[44] Morendo in grazia, etc. This quotation is incorrectly given in the 4to. It has been amended into impiety, for which there is little occasion. We have already seen more than enough to prove that when a woman loses the sense of religion, (and Annabella, like her brother, is a fatalist,) modesty, self-respect, every virtuous, and every amiable feeling speedily follow.

Soranzo. Dost thou triumph? the treasure of the earth
Shall not redeem thee; were there kneeling kings
Did beg thy life, or angels did come down
To plead in tears, yet should not all prevail
Against my rage: dost thou not tremble yet?

Annabella. At what? to die! no, be a gallant hangman;
I dare thee to the worst: strike, and strike home;
I leave revenge behind, and thou shalt feel it.

Soranzo. Yet tell me ere thou diest, and tell me truly,
Knows thy old father this?

Annabella. No, by my life.

Soranzo. Wilt thou confess, and I will spare thy life?

Annabella. My life! I will not buy my life so dear.

Soranzo. I will not slack my vengeance. [Draws his sword.

Enter Vasques.

Vasques. What do you mean, sir?

Soranzo. Forbear, Vasques; such a damned whore Deserves no pity.

Vasques. Now the gods forefend! And would you be her executioner, and
kill her in your rage too? O 'twere most unmanlike; she is your wife,
what faults have been done by her before she married you, were not
against you: alas! poor lady, what hath she committed, which any lady
in Italy in the like case would not? sir, you must be ruled by your
reason, and not by your fury; that were inhuman and beastly.

Soranzo. She shall not live.

Vasques. Come, she must: you would have her confess the authors of her
present misfortunes, I warrant you; 'tis an unconscionable demand,
and she should lose the estimation that I, for my part, hold of her
worth, if she had done it: why, sir, you ought not, of all men living, to
know it. Good sir, be reconciled; alas, good gentlewoman!

Annabella. Pish, do not beg for me, I prize my life
     As nothing; if the man will needs be mad,
     Why let him take it.

Soranzo. Vasques, hear'st thou this?

Vasques. Yes, and commend her for it[45]; in this she shews the nobleness of
     a gallant spirit, and be — shrew my heart, but it becomes her rarely.
     — [*Aside to Sor.*] — Sir, in any case smother your revenge; leave the
     scenting out your wrongs to me; be ruled, as you respect your
     honour, or you marr all. —[*Aloud.*]— Sir, if ever my service were of
     any credit with you, be not so violent in your distractions: you are
     married now; what a triumph might the report of this give to other
     neglected suitors! 'tis as manlike to bear extremities, as godlike to
     forgive.

Soranzo. O Vasques, Vasques, in this piece of flesh,
     This faithless face of hers, had I laid up
     The treasure of my heart. Hadst thou been virtuous,
     Fair, wicked woman, not the matchless joys
     Of life itself, had made me wish to live
     With any saint but thee: deceitful creature,
     How hast thou mock'd my hopes, and in the shame
     Of thy lewd womb even buried me alive!
     I did too dearly love thee.

Vasques. This is well; follow this temper with some passion; be brief and
     moving, 'tis for the purpose.
Aside to Sor.

Soranzo. Be witness to my words thy soul and thoughts;
     And tell me, didst not think that in my heart
     I did too superstitiously adore thee?

Annabella. I must confess, I know you lov'd me well.

Soranzo. And would'st thou use me thus! O Annabella,
     Be thou assured, whoe'er the villain was
     That thus hath tempted thee to this disgrace,

---

[45] This odious wretch has no variety in his bloody tricks: here is a repetition of the paltry artificehy which Hippolita was deceived; and Putuna is subsequently wrought upon much in the same manner. Vasques is fortunate in finding suet easy gulls.

Well he might lust, but never loved like me.
He doated on the picture that hung out
Upon thy cheeks, to please his humorous eye;
Not on the part I lov'd, which was thy heart,
And, as I thought, thy virtues.

Annabella. O, my lord!
These words wound deeper than your sword could do.

Vasques. Let me not ever take comfort, but I begin to weep myself, so much
I pity him; why, madam, I knew, when his rage was over-past, what it
would come to.

Soranzo. Forgive me, Annabella: though thy youth
Hath tempted thee above thy strength to folly,
Yet will I not forget what I should be,
And what I am, a husband; in that name
Is hid divinity: if I do find
That thou wilt yet be true, here I remit
All former faults, and take thee to my bosom.

Vasques. By my troth, and that's a point of noble charity.

Annabella. Sir, on my knees —

Soranzo. Rise up, you shall not kneel.
Get you to your chamber, see you make no shew
Of alteration; I'll be with you straight:
My reason tells me now, that "'tis as common
To err in frailty as to be a woman."
Go to your chamber.
Exit Ann.

Vasques. So! this was somewhat to the matter: what do you think of your
heaven of happiness now, sir?

Soranzo. I carry hell about me, all my blood
Is fired in swift revenge.

Vasques. That may be; but know you how, or on whom? Alas! to marry a
great woman, being made great in the stock to your hand, is a usual

sport in these days; but to know what ferret it was[46] that hunted your coney-burrow — there is the cunning.

Soranzo. I'll make her tell herself, or —

Vasques. Or what? you must not do so; let me yet persuade your sufferance a little while: go to her, use her mildly; win her, if it be possible, to a voluntary, to a weeping tune; for the rest, if all hit, I will not miss my mark. Pray, sir, go in; the next news I tell you shall be wonders.

Soranzo. Delay in vengeance gives a heavier blow.
Exit.

Vasques. Ah, sirrah, here's work for the nonce! I had a suspicion of a bad matter in my head a pretty while ago; but after my madam's scurvy looks here at home, her waspish perverseness, and loud fault-finding, then I remembered the proverb,that "where hens crow, and cocks hold their peace, there are sorry houses." 'Sfoot, if the lower parts of a she-tailor's cunning can cover such a swelling in the stomach, I'll never blame a false stitch in a shoe whilst I live again. Up, and up so quick? and so quickly too? 'twere a fine policy to learn by whom: this must be known; and I have thought on't —

Enter Putana, in tears.

Here's the way, or none. — What, crying, old mistress! alas, alas, I cannot blame you; we have a lord, Heaven help us, is so mad as the devil himself, the more shame for him.

Putana. O Vasques, that ever I was born to see this day! Doth he use thee so too, sometimes, Vasques?

Vasques. Me? why he makes a dog of me; but if some were of my mind, I know what we would do. As sure as I am an honest man, he will ge near to kill my lady with unkindness: say she be with child, is that such a matter for a young woman of her years to be blamed for?

Putana. Alas, good heart, it is against her will full sore.

---

[46] to know what ferret it was. This is the ingenious emendation of Dodsley. The 4to reads secret; and it may be conjectured that the substantive which probably followed it has been lost. The present reading, however, leaves nothing to regret.

Vasques. I durst be sworn, all his madness is for that she will not confess whose 'tis, which he will know; and when he doth know it, I am so well acquainted with his humour, that he will forget all strait: well, I could wish she would in plain terms tell all, for that's the way, indeed.

Putana. Do you think so?

Vasques. Foh, I know it; provided that he did not win her to it by force. He was once in a mind that you could tell, and meant to have wrung it out of you; but I somewhat pacified him from that; yet sure you know a great deal.

Putana. Heaven forgive us all! I know a little, Vasques.

Vasques. Why should you not? who else should? Upon my conscience she loves you dearly; and you would not betray her to any affliction for the world.

Putana. Not for all the world, by my faith and troth, Vasques.

Vasques. Twere pity of your life if you should; but in this you should both relieve her present discomforts, pacify my lord, and gain yourself everlasting love and preferment.

Putana. Dost think so, Vasques?

Vasques. Nay, I know it; sure it was some near and entire friend.

Putana. Twas a dear friend indeed; but —

Vasques. But what? fear not to name him; my life between you and danger: 'faith, I think it was no base fellow.

Putana. Thou wilt stand between me and harm?

Vasques. U'ds pity, what else? you shall be rewarded too, trust me.

Putana. Twas even no worse than her own brother.

Vasques. Her brother Giovanni, I warrant you!

Putana. Even he, Vasques; as brave a gentleman as ever kiss'd fair lady. O they love most perpetually.

Vasques. A brave gentleman indeed! why therein I commend her choice —
better and better — [Aside.] You are sure 'twas he?

Putana. Sure; and you shall see he will not be long from her too.

Vasques. He were to blame if he would; but may I believe thee?

Putana. Believe me! why, dost think I am a Turk or a Jew? No, Vasques, I
have known their dealings too long, to belie them now.

Vasques. Where are you? there, within, sirs!

Enter Banditti.[47]

Putana. How now, what are these?

Vasques. You shall know presently. Come, sirs, take me this old damnable
hag, gag her instantly, and put out her eyes, quickly, quickly!

Putana. Vasques! Vasques!

Vasques. Gag her, I say; 'sfoot, do you suffer her to prate? what do you
fumble about? let me come to her. I'll help your old gums, you toad-
bellied bitch! [*they gag her.*] Sirs, carry her closely into the coal-house,
and put out her eyes instantly; if she roars, slit her nose; do you hear,
be speedy and sure. [*Exeunt Banditti with Putana.*]

Why this is excellent, and above expectation — her own brother! O
horrible! to what a height of liberty in damnation hath the devil
trained our age! her brother, well! there's yet but a beginning; I must
to my lord, and tutor him better in his points of vengeance: now I see
how a smooth tale goes beyond a smooth tail; but soft — what thing
comes next? Giovanni! as I could wish; my belief is strengthened, 'tis
as firm as winter and summer.

Enter Giovanni.

Giovanni. Where's my sister?

---

[47] Enter Banditti. It may appear singular, that Vasques should have a body of assassins
awaiting his call; before he had any assurance that they would be needed; the circumstance
serves, however, to illustrate the savage nature of this revengeful villain.

Vasques. Troubled with a new sickness, my lord; she's somewhat ill.

Giovanni. Took too much of the flesh, I believe.

Vasques. Troth, sir, and you I think have even hit it; but my virtuous lady —

Giovanni. Where is she?

Vasques. In her chamber; please you visit her; she is alone. [*Gio. gives him money.*] Your liberality hath doubly made me your servant, and ever shall, ever [*Exit Gio.*]

Re-enter Soranzo.

Sir, I am made a man; I have plied my cue with cunning and success; I beseech you let us be private.

Soranzo. My lady's brother's come; now he'll know all.

Vasques. Let him know it; I have made some of them fast enough. How have you dealt with my lady?

Soranzo. Gently, as thou hast counsell'd; O my soul
Runs circular in sorrow for revenge;
But, Vasques, thou shalt know

Vasques. Nay, I will know no more, for now comes your turn to know; I would not talk so openly with you — let my young master take time enough, and go at pleasure; he is sold to death, and the devil shall not ransom him. — Sir, I beseech you, your privacy.

Soranzo. No conquest can gain glory of my fear.

Exeunt.

ACT V.
SCENE I.

The Street before Soranzo's House.

Annabella appears at a Window, above.

Annabella. Pleasures, farewell, and all ye thriftless minutes
       Wherein false joys have spun a weary life!
       To these my fortunes now I take my leave.
       Thou, precious Time, that swiftly rid'st in post
       Over the world, to finish up the race
       Of my last fate, here stay thy restless course,
       And bear to ages that are yet unborn
       A wretched, woeful woman's tragedy!
       My conscience now stands up against my lust,
       With depositions character'd in guilt,

Enter Friar, below.

       And tells me I am lost: now I confess;
       Beauty that clothes the outside of the face,
       Is cursed if it be not cloth'd with grace.
       Here like a turtle, (mew'd up in a cage,)
       Unmated, I converse with air and walls,
       And descant on my vile unhappiness.
       O Giovanni, that hast had the spoil
       Of thine own virtues, and my modest fame;
       Would thou hadst been less subject to those stars
       That luckless reign'd at my nativity!
       O would the scourge, due to my black offence,
       Might pass from thee, that I alone might feel
       The torment of an uncontrouled flame!

Friar. What's this I hear?

Annabella. That man, that blessed friar,
       Who join'd in ceremonial knot my hand
       To him whose wife I now am, told me oft,
       I trod the path to death, and shew'd me how.
       But they who sleep in lethargies of lust,
       Hug their confusion, making Heaven unjust;
       And so did I.

Friar. Here's music to the soul!

Annabella. Forgive me, my good Genius, and this once
        Be helpful to my ends; let some good man
        Pass this way, to whose trust I may commit
        This paper, double lined with tears and blood;
        Which being granted, here I sadly vow
        Repentance, and a leaving of that life
        I long have died in.

Friar. Lady, Heaven hath heard you,
        And hath by providence ordain'd, that I
        Should be his minister for your behoof.

Annabella. Ha, what are you?

Friar. Your brother's friend, the Friar;
        Glad in my soul that I have liv'd to hear
        This free confession 'twixt your peace and you:
        What would you, or to whom? fear not to speak.

Annabella. Is Heaven so bountiful? — then I have found
        More favour than I hoped; here, holy man —
Throws down a letter.
        Commend me to my brother, give him that,
        That letter; bid him read it, and repent.
        Tell him that I, imprison'd in my chamber,
        Barr'd of all company, even of my guardian,
        (Which gives me cause of much suspect) have time
        To blush at what hath past; bid him be wise,
        And not believe the friendship of my lord;
        I fear much more than I can speak: good father,
        The place is dangerous, and spies are busy.
        I must break off. — you'll do't?

Friar. Be sure I will,
        And fly with speed: my blessing ever rest
        With thee, my daughter; live, to die more blest!
Exit.

Annabella. Thanks to the heavens, who have prolong'd my breath
        To this good use! now I can welcome death.

Withdraws from the window.

SCENE II.

Another Room in the same.

Enter Soranzo and Vasques.

Vasques. Am I to be believed now? first, marry a strumpet that cast herself
away upon you but to laugh at your horns! to feast on your disgrace,
riot in your vexations, cuckold you in your bride — bed, waste your
estate upon panders and bawds! —

Soranzo. No more, I say, no more.

Vasques. A cuckold is a goodly tame beast, my lord!

Soranzo. I am resolv'd; urge not another word;
My thoughts are great, and all as resolute
As thunder; in mean time, I'll cause our lady
To deck herself in all her bridal robes;
Kiss her, and fold her gently in my arms.
Begone — yet hear you, are the banditti ready
To wait in ambush?

Vasques. Good sir, trouble not yourself about other business than your own
resolution; remember that time lost cannot be recalled.

Soranzo. With all the cunning words thou canst, invite
The states of Parma to my birth-day's feast:
Haste to my brother-rival and his father,
Entreat them gently, bid them not to fail;
Be speedy, and return.

Vasques. Let not your pity betray you, till my coming back; think upon incest
and cuckoldry.

Soranzo. Revenge is all the ambition I aspire,
To that I'll climb or fall; my blood's on fire.

Exeunt.

SCENE III.

A Room in Florio's House.

Enter Giovanni.

Giovanni. Busy opinion is an idle fool,
   That, as a school-rod keeps a child in awe,
   Frights th' unexperienced temper of the mind:
   So did it me; who, ere my precious sister
   Was married, thought all taste of love would die
   In such a contract; but I find no change
   Of pleasure in this formal law of sports.
   She is still one to me, and every kiss
   As sweet and as delicious as the first
   I reap'd, when yet the privilege of youth
   Entitled her a virgin. O the glory;
   Of two united hearts like hers and mine!
   Let poring book-men dream of other worlds;
   My world, and all of happiness, is here,
   And I'd not change it for the best to come:
   A life of pleasure is Elysium.

Enter Friar.

   Father, you enter on the jubilee
   Of my retired delights; now I can tell you,
   The hell you oft have prompted, is nought else
   But slavish and fond superstitious fear;
   And I could prove it too

Friar. Thy blindness slays thee:
   Look there, 'tis writ to thee. [Gives him the letter.

Giovanni. From whom?

Friar. Unrip the seals and see;
   The blood's yet seething hot, that will anon
   Be frozen harder than congealed coral. —
   Why d'ye change colour, son?

Giovanni. 'Fore heaven, you make
   Some petty devil factor 'twixt my love
   And your religion-masked sorceries.

Where had you this?

Friar. Thy conscience, youth, is sear'd,
      Else thou would'st stoop to warning.

Giovanni. Tis her hand,
      I know't; and 'tis all written in her blood.
      She writes I know not what. Death! I'll not fear
      An armed thunderbolt aim'd at my heart.
      She writes, we are discover'd — pox on dreams
      Of low faint-hearted cowardice! — discover'd?
      The devil we are! which way is't possible?
      Are we grown traitors to our own delights?
      Confusion take such dotage! 'tis but forged;
      This is your peevish chattering, weak old man! —
      Now, sir, what news bring you?

Enter Vasques.

Vasques. My lord, according to his yearly custom, keeping this day a feast in honour of his birthday, by me invites you thither. Your worthy father, with the pope's reverend nuncio, and other magnificoes of Parma, have promised their presence; will't please you to be of the number?

Giovanni. Yes, tell [him] I dare come.

Vasques. Dare come?

Giovanni. So I said; and tell him more, I will come.

Vasques. These words are strange to me.

Giovanni. Say, I will come.

Vasques. You will not miss?

Giovanni. Yet more! I'll come, sir. Are you answered?

Vasques. So I'll say my service to you. [Exit.

Friar. You will not go, I trust.

Giovanni. Not go! for what?

Friar. O, do not go; this feast, I'll gage my life,
      Is but a plot to train you to your ruin;
      Be ruled, you shall not go.

Giovanni. Not go! stood death
      Threatening his armies of confounding plagues,
      With hosts of dangers hot as blazing stars,
      I would be there; not go! yes, and resolve
      To strike as deep in slaughter as they all;
      For I will go.

Friar. Go where thou wilt; — I see
      The wildness of thy fate draws to an end,
      To a bad fearful end:— I must not stay
      To know thy fall; back to Bononia I
      With speed will haste, and shun this coming blow.
      Parma, farewell; would I had never known thee,
      Or aught of thine! Well, young man, since no prayer
      Can make thee safe, I leave thee to despair. [*Exit.*

Giovanni. Despair, or tortures of a thousand hells,
      All's one to me; I have set up my rest.[48]
      Now, now, work serious thoughts on baneful plots;
      Be all a man, my soul; let not the curse
      Of old prescription rend from me the gall
      Of courage, which enrolls a glorious death:
      If I must totter like a well-grown oak,
      Some under-shrubs shall in my weighty fall
      Be crush'd to splits; with me they all shall perish!

Exit.

---

[48] I have set up my rest. i.e. I have made my determination; taken my fixed and final resolution.

SCENE IV.

A Hall in Soranzo's Home.

Enter Soranzo, Vasques with Masks, and Banditti.

Soranzo. You will not fail, or shrink in the attempt?

Vasques. I will undertake for their parts; be sure, my masters, to be bloody enough, and as unmerciful as if you were preying upon a rich booty oh the very mountains of Liguria: for your pardons, trust to my lord; but for reward, you shall trust none but your own pockets.

Banditti. We'll make a murder.

Soranzo. Here's gold — [*Gives them money*]— here's more; want nothing; what you do
Is noble, and an act of brave revenge:
I'll make you rich, banditti, and all free.

Omnes. Liberty! liberty!

Vasques. Hold, take every man a vizard; when you are withdrawn, keep as much silence as you can possibly. You know the watch-word,[49] till which be spoken, move not; but when you hear that, rush in like a stormy flood: I need not instruct you in your own profession.

Omnes. No, no, no.

Vasques. In, then; your ends are profit and preferment. — Away!
Exeunt Ban.

Soranzo. The guests will all come, Vasques?

Vasques. Yes, sir. And now let me a little edge your resolution: you see nothing is unready to this great work, but a great mind in you; call to your remembrance your disgraces, your loss of honour, Hippolita's blood, and arm your courage in your own wrongs; so shall you best right those wrongs in vengeance, which you may truly call your own.

---

[49] You know the watch-word. It appears, from a subsequent passage, that this was "Vengeance."

Soranzo. 'Tis well; the less I speak, the more I burn,
    And blood shall quench that flame.

Vasques. Now you begin to turn Italian. This beside; when my young incest-
    monger comes, he will be sharp set on his old bit: give him time
    enough, let him have your chamber and bed at liberty; let my hot
    hare have law ere he be hunted to his death, that, if it be possible, he
    post to hell in the very act of his damnation[50].

Soranzo. It shall be so; and see, as we would wish, He comes himself first —

Enter Giovanni.

    Welcome, my much-lov'd brother;
    Now I perceive you honour me; you are welcome —
    But where's my father?

Giovanni. With the other states,
    Attending on the nuncio of the pope,
    To wait upon him hither. How's my sister?

Soranzo. Like a good housewife, scarcely ready yet;
    You were best walk to her chamber.

Giovanni. If you will.

Soranzo. I must expect my honourable friends;
    Good brother, get her forth.

Giovanni. You are busy, sir.
Exit.

Vasques. Even as the great devil himself would have it! let him go and glut
    himself in his own destruction —[*Flourish.*]— Hark, the nuncio is at
    hand; good sir, be ready to receive him.

Enter Cardinal, Florio, Donado, Richardetto, and Attendants.

---

[50] That, if it be possible, he post to hell in the very act of his damnation. This infernal sentiment has been copied from Shakspeare by several writers who were nearly his contemporaries. — Reed. It is not, however, ill placed in the mouth of such an incarnate fiend as Vasques.

Soranzo. Most reverend lord, this grace hath made me proud,
   That you vouchsafe my house; I ever rest
   Your humble servant for this noble favour.

Cardinal. You are our friend, my lord; his Holiness
   Shall understand how zealously you honour
   Saint Peter's vicar in his substitute:
   Our special love to you.

Soranzo. Signiors, to you
   My welcome, and my ever best of thanks
   For this so memorable courtesy.
   Pleaseth your grace walk near?

Cardinal. My lord, we come
   To celebrate your feast with civil mirth,
   As ancient custom teacheth: we will go.

Soranzo. Attend his grace there. Signiors, keep your way.

Exeunt.

SCENE V.

Annabella's Bed Chamber in the same.

Annabella, richly dressed, and Giovanni.

Giovanni. What, chang'd so soon! hath your new sprightly lord
       Found out a trick in night-games more than we
       Could know, in our simplicity? — Ha! is't so?
       Or does the fit come on you, to prove treacherous
       To your past vows and oaths?

Annabella. Why should you jest
       At my calamity, without all sense
       Of the approaching dangers you are in?

Giovanni. What danger's half so great as thy revolt?
       Thou art a faithless sister, else thou know'st,
       Malice, or any treachery beside,
       Would stoop to my bent brows; why, I hold fate
       Clasp'd in my fist, and could command the course
       Of time's eternal motion, hadst thou been
       One thought more steady than an ebbing sea.
       And what? you'll now be honest, that's resolv'd?

Annabella. Brother, dear brother, know what I have been,
       And know that now there's but a dining-time
       'Twixt us and our confusion; let's not waste
       These precious hours in vain and useless speech.
       Alas! these gay attires were not put on
       But to some end; this sudden solemn feast
       Was not ordain'd to riot in expense;
       I that have now been chamber'd here alone,
       Barr'd of my guardian, or of any else,
       Am not for nothing at an instant freed
       To fresh access. Be not deceiv'd, my brother,
       This banquet is an harbinger of death
       To you and me; resolve yourself it is,
       And be prepared to welcome it.

Giovanni. Well, then;
       The schoolmen teach that all this globe of earth
       Shall be consumed to ashes in a minute.

Annabella. So I have read too.

Giovanni. But 'twere somewhat strange
        To see the waters burn; could I believe
        This might be true, I could believe as well
        There might be hell or heaven.

Annabella. That's most certain.

Giovanni. A dream, a dream! else in this other world
        We should know one another.

Annabella. So we shall.

Giovanni. Have you heard so?

Annabella. For certain.

Giovanni. But do you think,
        That I shall see you there? You look on me.[51] —
        May we kiss one another, prate or laugh,
        Or do as we do here?

Annabella. I know not that;
        But — brother, for the present, what d'ye mean[52]
        To free yourself from danger? some way think
        How to escape; I'm sure the guests are come.

Giovanni. Look up, look here; what see you in my face?

Annabella. Distraction and a troubled conscience.[53]

Giovanni. Death, and a swift repining wrath:— yet look;
        What see you in mine eyes?

Annabella. Methinks you weep.

---

[51] You look on me. i. e. You look with surprize or astonishment on me. Such is the force of this expression.

[52] But — brother, for the present, what d'ye mean. The 4to, which is imperfect in this place, reads, "But good for the present." The word adopted is certainly not the author's; but it is safe, at least; and I prefer it to inserting a monosyllable at random.

[53] Distraction and a troubled conscience. The old copy reads a troubled countenance; well corrected by Dodsley.

Giovanni. I do indeed; these are the funeral tears
    Shed on your grave; these furrow'd up my cheeks
    When first I lov'd and knew not how to woo.
    Fair Annabella, should I here repeat
    The story of my life, we might lose time.
    Be record all the spirits of the air,
    And all things else that are, that day and night,
    Early and late, the tribute which my heart
    Hath paid to Annabella's sacred love,
    Hath been these tears, which are her mourners now!
    Never till now did nature do her best,
    To shew a matchless beauty to the world,
    Which in an instant, ere it scarce was seen,
    The jealous destinies required again.
    Pray, Annabella, pray! since we must part,
    Go thou, white in thy soul, to fill a throne
    Of innocence and sanctity in heaven.
    Pray, pray, my sister!

Annabella. Then I see your drift —
Ye blessed angels, guard me!

Giovanni. So say I;
    Kiss me. If ever after-times should hear
    Of our fast-knit affections, though perhaps
    The laws of conscience and of civil use
    May justly blame us, yet when they but know
    Our loves, that love will wipe away that rigour,
    Which would in other incests be abhorr'd.
    Give me your hand: how sweetly life doth run
    In these well-colour'd veins! how constantly
    These palms do promise health! but I could chide
    With nature for this cunning flattery —
    Kiss me again — forgive me.

Annabella. With my heart.

Giovanni. Farewell!

Annabella. Will you be gone?

Giovanni. Be dark, bright sun,
    And make this mid-day night, that thy gilt rays

May not behold a deed, will turn their splendour
More sooty than the poets feign their Styx!
One other kiss, my sister.

Annabella. What means this?

Giovanni. To save thy fame, and kill thee in a kiss.
Stabs her.
Thus die, and die by me, and by my hand!
Revenge is mine; honour doth love command.

Annabella. Oh brother, by your hand!

Giovanni. When thou art dead I'll give my reasons for't; for to dispute
With thy (even in thy death) most lovely beauty,
Would make me stagger to perform this act
Which I most glory in.

Annabella. Forgive him, Heaven — and me my sins! farewell,
Brother unkind, unkind — mercy, great Heaven! oh — oh!
Dies.

Giovanni. She's dead, alas, good soul! The hapless fruit
That in her womb received its life from me,
Hath had from me a cradle and a grave.
I must not dally — this sad marriage-bed
In all her best, bore her alive and dead.
Soranzo, thou hast miss'd thy aim in this!
I have prevented now thy reaching plots,
And kill'd a love, for whose each drop of blood
I would have pawn'd my heart. Fair Annabella,
How over-glorious art thou in thy wounds,
Triumphing over infamy and hate!
Shrink not, courageous hand, stand up, my heart,
And boldly act my last, and greater part!

The scene closes.

SCENE VI.

A Banquetting Room in the same.[54]

A Banquet. — Enter the Cardinal, Florio, Donado, Soranzo, Richardetto, Vasques, and Attendants.

Vasques. [*apart to Sor.*] Remember, sir, what you have to do; be wise and
    resolute.

Soranzo. Enough — my heart is fix'd. — Pleaseth your grace
    To taste these coarse confections: though the use
    Of such set entertainments more consists
    In custom, than in cause, yet, reverend sir,
    I am still made your servant by your presence.

Cardinal. And we your friend.

Soranzo. But where's my brother Giovanni?

Enter Giovanni, with a Heart upon his Dagger.

Giovanni. Here, here, Soranzo! trimm'd in reeking blood,
    That triumphs over death! proud in the spoil
    Of love and vengeance! fate, or all the powers
    That guide the motions of immortal souls,
    Could not prevent me.

Cardinal. What means this?

Florio. Son Giovanni!

Soranzo. Shall I be forestall'd? [Aside.

Giovanni. Be not amaz'd: if your misgiving hearts
    Shrink at an idle sight, what bloodless fear
    Of coward passion would have seiz'd your senses,
    Had you beheld the rape of life and beauty
    Which I have acted? — my sister, oh my sister!

---

[54] A banquetting room. They had dined in another room, and, according to the usual practice, repaired to the apartment in which the confectionery was set out.

Florio. Ha! what of her?

Giovanni. The glory of my deed
       Darken'd the mid-day sun, made noon as night.
       You came to feast, my lords, with dainty fare,
       I came to feast too; but I digg'd for food
       In a much richer mine, than gold or stone
       Of any value balanced; 'tis a heart,
       A heart, my lords, in which is mine entomb'd:
       Look well upon't; do you know it?

Vasques. What strange riddle's this?
Aside.

Giovanni. Tis Annabella's heart, 'tis; why do you startle?
       I vow 'tis her's; — this dagger's point plough'd up
       Her fruitful womb, and left to me the fame
       Of a most glorious executioner.

Florio. Why, madman, art thyself?

Giovanni. Yes, father; and, that times to come may know,
       How, as my fate, I honour'd my revenge,
       List, father; to your ears I will yield up
       How much I have deserv'd to be your son.

Florio. What is't thou say'st?

Giovanni. Nine moons have had their changes,
       Since I first thoroughly view'd, and truly lov'd,
       Your daughter and my sister.

Florio. How? Alas, my lords, He is a frantic madman!

Giovanni. Father, no.
       For nine months space, in secret, I enjoy'd
       Sweet Annabella's sheets; nine months I lived
       A happy monarch of her heart and her;
       Soranzo, thou know'st this; thy paler cheek
       Bears the confounding print of thy disgrace;
       For her too fruitful womb too soon bewray'd
       The happy passage of our stolen delights,
       And made her mother to a child unborn.

Cardinal. Incestuous villain!

Florio. Oh, his rage belies him.

Giovanni. It does not, 'tis the oracle of truth;
       I vow it is so.

Soranzo. I shall burst with fury —
       Bring the strumpet forth!

Vasques. I shall, sir.
Exit.

Giovanni. Do, sir; have you all no faith
       To credit yet my triumphs? here I swear
       By all that you call sacred, by the love
       I bore my Annabella whilst she lived,
       These hands have from her bosom ripp'd this heart.

Re-enter Vasques.

       Is't true or no, sir?

Vasques. Tis most strangely true.

Florio. Cursed man — have I lived to — [*Dies.*]

Cardinal. Hold up, Florio.
       Monster of children! see what thou hast done,
       Broke thy old father's heart! is none of you
       Dares venture on him?

Giovanni. Let them! Oh my father,
       How well his death becomes him in his griefs!
       Why this was done with courage; now survives
       None of our house but I, gilt in the blood
       Of a fair sister and a hapless father.

Soranzo. Inhuman scorn of men, hast thou a thought
       T' outlive thy murders? [*Draws.*]

Giovanni. Yes, I tell thee yes;

For in my fists I bear the twists of life.
Soranzo, see this heart, which was thy wife's;
Thus I exchange it royally for thine, [*They fight.*]
And thus and thus! now brave revenge is mine.
Soranzo falls.

Vasques. I cannot hold any longer. You, sir, are you grown insolent in your
butcheries? have at you.

Giovanni. Come, I am arm'd to meet thee. [*They fight.*]

Vasques. No! will it not be yet? if this will not, another shall. Not yet? I shall
fit you anon — Vengeance![55]

The Banditti rush in.

Giovanni. Welcome! come more of you; whate'er you be,
    I dare your worst
[*They surround and wound him.*]
        Oh I can stand no longer; feeble arms,
        Have you so soon lost strength? [*Falls.*]

Vasques. Now, you are welcome, sir! — Away, my masters, all is done; shift
for yourselves, your reward is your own: shift for yourselves. [Aside
to Band.

Banditti. Away, away! [*Exeunt.*]

Vasques. How do you, my lord? See you this? [*pointing to Gio.*] how is't?

Soranzo. Dead; but in death well pleas'd, that I have liv'd
        To see my wrongs reveng'd on that black devil.
        O Vasques, to thy bosom let me give
        My last of breath; let not that lecher live —
        Oh! — [*Dies.*]

Vasques. The reward of peace and rest be with [you], my ever dearest lord
and master!

---

[55] Vengeance! This, as was observed, was the watch-word or preconcerted signal for
assistance.

Giovanni. Whose hand gave me this wound?

Vasques. Mine, sir; I was your first man; have you enough?

Giovanni. I thank thee, thou hast done for me
But what I would have else done on myself.
Art sure thy lord is dead? —

Vasques. Oh impudent slave!
As sure as I am sure to see thee die.

Cardinal. Think on thy life and end, and call for mercy.

Giovanni. Mercy? why, I have found it in this justice.

Cardinal. Strive yet to cry to Heaven.

Giovanni. Oh I bleed fast.
Death, thou'rt a guest long look'd for, I embrace
Thee and thy wounds; oh, my last minute comes!
Where'er I go, let me enjoy this grace,
Freely to view my Annabella's face. [*Dies.*]

Donado. Strange miracle of justice!

Cardinal. Raise up the city, we shall be murder'd all!

Vasques. You need not fear, you shall not; this strange task being ended, I
have paid the duty to the son, which I have vowed to the father.

Cardinal. Speak, wretched villain, what incarnate fiend
Hath led thee on to this?

Vasques. Honesty, and pity of my master's wrongs: for know, my lord, I am
by birth a Spaniard, brought forth my country in my youth by lord
Soranzo's father; whom, whilst he lived, I served faithfully; since
whose death I have been to this man, as I was to him. What I have
done, was duty, and I repent nothing, but that the loss of my life had
not ransomed his.

Cardinal. Say, fellow, know'st thou any yet unnam'd, Of council in this
incest?

Vasques. Yes, an old woman, sometime guardian to this murder'd lady.

Cardinal. And what's become of her?

Vasques. Within this room she is; whose eyes, after her confession, I caused
       to be put out, but kept alive, to confirm what from Giovanni's own
       mouth you have heard. Now, my lord, what I have done you may
       judge of; and let your own wisdom be a judge in your own reason.

Cardinal. Peace! first this woman,[56] chief in these effects,
       My sentence is, that forthwith she be ta'en
       Out of the city, for example's sake,
       There to be burnt to ashes.

Donado. 'Tis most just.

Cardinal. Be it your charge, Donado, see it done.

Donado. I shall.

Vasques. What for me? if death, 'tis welcome; I have been honest to the son,
       as I was to the father.

Cardinal. Fellow, for thee, since what thou didst was done
       Not for thyself, being no Italian,
       We banish thee for ever; to depart
       Within three days: in this we do dispense
       With grounds of reason, not of thine offence.

Vasques. 'Tis well; this conquest is mine, and I rejoice that a Spaniard
       outwent an Italian in revenge. [Exit.

Cardinal. Take up these slaughter'd bodies, see them buried;
       And all the gold and jewels, or whatsoever,
       Confiscate by the canons of the church,
       We seize upon to the Pope's proper use.

---

[56] First this woman, etc. What! without hearing her? It is well, however, that some one was at hand to satisfy the Cardinal's fierce love of justice. The sacrifice, it must be confessed, is somewhat like that of the poor bed-rid weaver in Hudibras; and if, of the four who now remain alive upon the stage, three, including his Eminence, had heen sentenced to the hurdle with her, few would have thought them too hardly dealt with.

Richardetto. [*Discovers himself.*] Your grace's pardon; thus long I liv'd
      disguised,
      To see the effect of pride and lust at once
      Brought both to shameful ends.

Cardinal. What! Richardetto, whom we thought for dead?

Donado. Sir, was it you

Richardetto. Your friend.

Cardinal. We shall have time
      To talk at large of all; but never yet
      Incest and murder have so strangely met.
      Of one so young, so rich in nature's store,
      Who could not say, 'Tis Pity She's A Whore?

Exeunt.

Here, instead of an Epilogue, we have, in the old copy, an apology for the errors of the press. It forms, as the learned Partridge says, a strange non sequitur; and is, in truth, more captious than logical. As a just compliment, however, to the skill of the performers, and the good taste of Lord Peterborough, it merits preservation. "The general commendation deserved by the actors in the presentment of this tragedy, may easily excuse such faults as are escaped in the printing. A common charity may allow him the ability of spelling, whom a secure confidence assures that he cannot ignorantly err in the application of sense."

The remarks on this dreadful story cannot be more appositely terminated, perhaps, than by the following passage from the concluding chapter of Sir Thomas Browne s Vulgar Errors. It is, as Mr. Lambe observes, "solemn and fine." "As there are many relations (he begins) whereto we cannot assent, and make some doubt thereof, so there are divers others whose verities we fear, and heartily wish there were no truth therein." — "For, of sins heteroclital, and such as want either name or precedent, there is oftimes a sin in their histories. We desire no records of such enormities; sins should be accounted new, that they may be esteemed monstrous. They omit of monstrosity, as they fall from their rarity; for men count it venial to err with their forefathers, and foolishly conceive they divide a sin in its society. The pens of men may sufficiently expatiate without these singularities of villainy; for as they increase the hatred of vice in some, so do they enlarge the theory of wickedness in all. And this is one thing that makes latter ages worse than were the former: for the vicious example of ages past poisons the curiosity of these present, affording a hint of sin unto seduceable spirits, and soliciting those unto the imitation of them, whose heads were never so perversely principled as to invent them. In things of this nature, silence com mendeth history; 'tis the veniable part of tilings lost, wherein there must never rise a Pancirollus, nor remain any register, but that of hell."

www.ingramcontent.com/pod-product-compliance
Lightning Source LLC
Chambersburg PA
CBHW071021120626
46546CB00003B/1183